HOW TO *BOOST* YOUR BRAIN POWER

THE PLAN FOR PEAK INTELLIGENCE, MEMORY AND CREATIVITY

ROGER B. YEPSEN, JR

THORSONS/RODALE

First published 1987

Copyright © 1987 by Rodale Press, Inc.

British Library Cataloguing in Publication Data

Yepsen, Roger B.
How to boost your brain power: a plan
for peak intelligence, memory and creativity.
1. Self-actualization (Psychology)
2. Mental discipline
I. Title
158'.1   BF637.S4

ISBN 0-7225-1522-7

Published by Thorsons Publishers Limited, Wellingborough, Northamptonshire, NN8 2RQ, England.

Printed and Bound in Great Britain by
Hartnolls Limited, Bodmin, Cornwall.

10 9 8 7 6 5

Contents

1

How Your
Brain Works
(or Doesn't)

The brain that processes these words as you read is *not* the one you were born with.

No, don't go rushing to a mirror to look for telltale scars around your temples. You still have the same brain cells you began life with, or most of them anyway. But your mind does change from day to day, even from hour to hour. You shape it unconsciously by eating, drinking, sleeping, and exercising, not to mention by thinking. All have their effects on the brain's chemical and physical makeup. You influenced your mind with the last meal you ate, and are doing so now as you read. This is remarkable news, in a couple of ways.

First, science until recently saw the brain as a self-contained machine of sorts, as the one organ that was independent of the body's ebb and flow of nutrients and oxygen. Now, research shows that the brain feels the effects of certain nutrients within minutes of a meal.

Second, science held that the brain grows rapidly during the first years of life and then, once we hit our twenties, settles down into a long, gradual slump. But research on aging has

---

Neuroterms

Neuro- is a prefix that pops up often in this book; it has to do with the nervous system. A neuron is a brain cell. Neurobiology, the study of the brain, has two branches: neuroanatomy, the study of the brain's structure; and neurophysiology, the study of the brain's function. A neurotransmitter is a naturally occurring chemical in the brain that either encourages or discourages the flow of electrical messages between neurons.

---

poked big holes in this scenario. Despite the grey view many of us have of growing older, our brains are not full-grown at the end of our teens, or at 40, or at 80 for that matter. Studies on laboratory animals suggest that the brain will continue to grow as long as the environment challenges and stimulates it. The brain is a "plastic" organ, as neuroanatomists put it, designed to expand its power to meet the demands we place upon it.

Of course, there are two sides to this newly discovered flexibility. What can be gained can be lost. Our mental powers are vulnerable to an indifferent diet. And they may wither through disuse, boredom, or a lack of self-confidence. "The brain, no less than the rest of the body, is subject to the 'use it or lose it' law," says Walter Bortz, M.D., president of the American Geriatrics Society and co-chairman of the American Medical Association's Committee on Aging. "As we allow ourselves to settle back into the brain-numbing existence found in many older [persons'] life patterns, senility cannot be far behind."

That fact puts a lot of responsibility on you, the owner-operator of a brain. This book can serve you as a practical guide to the mind's operation and maintenance. It's far from the first such book, of course. User's guides to the brain have been around at least since the phrenology manuals of the 1800s told readers they could chart intellectual zones by feeling bumps on a person's head. Traditionally, self-help books have been little more than extended pep talks, and they make use of the old "I *think* I can, I *think* I can" principle. But today, the outpouring of research into the mind yields all sorts of immediate, practical ways in which you can make the most of the brain's newly discovered ability to change and grow.

People rarely fail to reach a life goal because they're short on raw mental power. Rather, this power isn't applied for some reason. Just as a car becomes stranded if its wheels can't get traction on a snow-covered road, you spin your *mental* wheels when you are unable to focus on a project because of anxiety. Or, an ongoing lack of sleep, exercise, or sound nutrition may sap your mental vigor.

Some readers will turn to this book to make their memories more absorbent. Others will be curious about ways to limber up their creativity. The book shares current thinking on how your mind can be swayed by foods, exercise, the quantity and quality of sleep, the emotions, light and noise, pollution, and caffeine and alcohol. You'll read about techniques for getting the body to cooperate in mental work: biofeedback, relaxation, exercise, meditation, and aerobic workouts.

Any or all of these factors will help you make the most of the mental resources you were born with—an important point, given that you have the same brain that served your prehistoric, club-wielding ancestors. The difference between them and you isn't mental wattage: The difference is the environment in which your brain develops, and this environment is largely of your making.

Intellectual Fitness

A few years ago, a 65-year-old man ran a 26-mile-plus marathon in two hours and 50 minutes. His time would have won him the gold medal in the 1908 Olympics!

His effort was extraordinary, but the current fitness boom has many unsung heroes. Thousands of us have learned that our bodies are capable of feats which once would have been all but unthinkable for people our age. New ideas on training and new attitudes towards aging have made the difference.

But we've been slower to pick up the habit of *intellectual* fitness. Many older people who feel at home in running shoes and sweatsuits still are self-conscious about going back to school, or considering a career change, or taking up a musical instrument. Most of us seem to take seriously the old saw about losing countless brain cells each and every day.

Well, this is one old saying that happens to be true. And unlike cells elsewhere in the body, our brain cells aren't replaced. Fortunately, the important variable here isn't the number of cells, but the circuitry and chemistry that interconnect the billions that do stay aboard. The complexity of this intercellular switchboard is astounding: The average brain cell (or neuron) is linked to some 10,000 others, and some neurons may be patched into as many as 200,000.

This book shows how your activities and thoughts can keep this network sparking. You can choose to take advantage of the mind's newly discovered vulnerability to influences within the body and without. Scientists long assumed that nature would see to it that something so complex and vital as the brain would be sealed off from the rude jars and jolts of everyday life—much as a prized, hand-built clock is placed high upon the mantel.

They were wrong. The brain is indeed located high above the body, but it happens to be connected by a neck. And the neck links mind and body via nerves and the bloodstream. Nerves carry electrical impulses to and from the brain, of course, as is graphically demonstrated when you hit your thumb with a hammer. But only in recent years have researchers come to appreciate the importance of the second communication system, conducted by chemical messengers which travel in the bloodstream. These chemicals, called hormones, carry the brain's commands all over the body, and also relay information from the provinces back to the brain.

It seems that nature intentionally tied our minds and bodies together in this way. Richard J. Wurtman, M.D., professor of neuroendocrinology at MIT, suggests that the brain's sensitivity to substances flowing through the bloodstream enables it to monitor and regulate such cyclic activities as eating, sleeping, and sex. But a by-product of this close relationship is that, as the body goes, so goes the mind. You can be at your mental best only when your body is ticking along nicely as well. Therein lies the danger in trying to coax more out of your mind at your body's expense—such as by drinking coffee to stay alert, skipping sleep to finish a project, or relying on alcohol to coax new ideas along. These strategies eventually sabotage your thinking through the toll they exact on your body. You can't artificially improve your mental performance without taking time to let your body rest and rebuild.

In order to appreciate how your everyday actions can either sap your mental energy or add to it, we'll look briefly at the tiny transactions between brain cells that constitute thought.

First of all, there are lots of brain cells—perhaps 100 billion of them. This would suggest severe crowding within a brain that weighs just 3 pounds or so, but these cells are not simply packed cheek-to-jowl. They are strung together by electrical fibers. Fibers called dendrites being electrical impulses into the nerve cell, and fibers called axions carry signals from the cell to other neurons. Taken together, your neurons involve some 20 watts of electrical power—about the amount consumed by a rather dim light bulb.

Brain Chemicals

Electricity is only part of this story. That's because neurons are not simply wired up like so many Christmas tree lights. The circuits between each cell are broken by a minute gap, known as a synapse, and there are an estimated 100 trillion of them. The transmission of signals across this gap is controlled by a variety of brain chemicals, some 30 of them at last count. These chemical transmitters have the power to either facilitate or discourage the leap of a message. By flooding into the liquid-filled synapse, they moderate our thinking, our emotions, and our behavior.

All this would be so much neurobiology if it weren't for the fact that you can influence your inventory of specific transmitters.

Levels of several neurotransmitters fluctuate in the brain as levels of the nutrients they're made from go up and down in the blood. A typical reaction you may have experienced is feeling drowsy after a starchy meal. A plateful of mashed potatoes may make you feel like taking a nap because spuds and other carbohydrate-rich foods enable the brain to produce more serotonin, a neurotransmitter that retards brain-cell firing to cause a sensation of relaxation. Many foods contribute an effect, although the psychoactive nutrients are found in them in modest amounts. Chapter 2 discusses which foods provide the raw materials for transmitters, and suggests practical ways of taking advantage of this mind-body link.

Both depression and Parkinson's disease have been linked to a problem with transmitters at synapses, and drugs are sometimes prescribed to control neurotransmission. For example, the tricyclics are a group of antidepressant drugs that allow a neurotransmitter to work longer before being inactivated by naturally occurring substances. But tampering so powerfully with the brain's own chemistry can produce side effects; the tricyclics may cause drowsiness, dry mouth, and prolonged dilation of the pupils.

Other naturally occurring chemicals also play a role in regulating the brain. As mentioned earlier, hormones are chemical messengers that travel through the blood to regulate organs and tissues. The brain, acting through the pituitary gland, is itself the most important hormone-producing gland in the body. By releasing chemicals into the bloodstream, it can reach sites that are beyond the network of local nerves. For example, the brain liberates hormones that influence lymphocytes, the cells in the blood that give us immunity from disease.

Curiously, the brain itself can be influenced by the hormones it is responsible for releasing; some enter the brain to perform a double function as neurotransmitters. One such chemical is adrenaline, the so-called fight-or-flight hormone. It not only prepares the body for action (by speeding up the heart rate, rechanneling blood flow, and prompting the release of blood sugar from the liver), but also gears us up mentally, and focuses and narrows attention.

Another family of brain chemicals is the neuropeptides. They appear to prime the brain so that less of a particular transmitter is needed to set off the firing of brain cells. Peptides have been found to influence thirst, memory, and sexual behavior. Some peptides (known as endorphins) affect the experience of pain and pleasure, much like the drug morphine, and they have been called the body's own opiates. Peptides released during exercise are credited with causing the pleasant experience of "runner's high." Hypnosis and acupuncture may also liberate these natural painkillers. And, as further evidence of the intimate links between brain and body, neuropeptides that were first located in the digestive system have since been found in the brain, while those known to act as neurotransmitters later turned up in the digestive organs as well.

Work is underway to synthesize neuropeptides for use as drugs that can lengthen attention span, improve memory, and even increase the amount of information that the brain can take in from the eyes. In working on these so-called analogs, Lyle Miller, Ph.D., of the Biobehavioral Sciences Department of Boston University School of Medicine, has sampled some himself. He finds that they do not act like a high-powered drug, but produce effects that are subtle, short-lived, and not unlike experiences he occasionally has had when "straight."

As promising as the chemicals may sound, don't expect to find them on the drugstore shelf for a long while. Dr. Miller lists the reasons why: These analogs are expensive to produce with present methods; research money is less plentiful than it was a few years ago; and the chemicals' addictive potential and long-term effects have yet to be judged.

Mind and Body, or Mind/Body?

Discoveries of ties between the mind and body have led scientists in the West to conclude what Eastern thinkers have claimed all along: that mind and body are one, that conceiving boundaries between the two is not only artificial but also harmful to our identity and our health.

Now, health care professionals are trying to narrow the gap between soma (body) and psyche (mind) by forming new, hybrid disciplines which consider the whole person. These include behavioral medicine, psychosomatic medicine, holistic medicine, and somatic psychotherapies or psychotechnologies—a big word for the therapies that aid the mind through work on the body, such as massage. All are responses to the dawning

realization that mind and body are inextricably (and wondrous-
ly) linked. Neither can function well without the health of the
other.

Distinctions between mind and body are "meaningless and
out of date," says Yale psychiatry professor Morton F. Reiser,
M.D., in his book *Mind, Brain, Body* (Basic Books, 1984). He is
not comfortable with the adjective "psychosomatic" in
describing disease because it suggests that mind and body are
two independent realms. Dr. Reiser maintains that psychiatric
and medical disorders involve causes in both body and mind,
and the social sphere as well.

The diagram on page 9 shows some of the ways in which the
three realms—body, mind, and environment—relate with one
another. Note that the arrows form circles. These return loops
provide the brain with "feedback" on the impact of its commands through the body (and on the outside world as well).

These feedback loops are very important to the coordination of body and mind, in a couple of ways. One way can be
troublesome, causing the mind to continue maintaining the body
in a state of stress even after the stimulus is long gone. Here's
how this happens:

1. The mind perceives a threat, and rouses the body to meet
   this challenge by releasing chemical messengers.
2. These messengers also have the effect of stimulating the
   brain itself.
3. The stimulated brain may then continue to sound the
   alarm, even though the original threat is gone.
4. If the feedback loop isn't interrupted in some way (such as
   by a relaxation technique or taking a walk), then this
   self-perpetuating stress reaction may have harmful effects
   on the body, as well as jamming the circuits of the mind.

But feedback performs a very vital function, as well. It
keeps the mind in touch with the world, both inside the body
and outside. The loops on the map show how the brain monitors
and self-corrects its actions. As a simple example, your ears
relay to your brain the howl of a man whose foot you accidentally stepped on; the brain then directs your body to remove the
foot. The brain can sense far more subtle states within the body

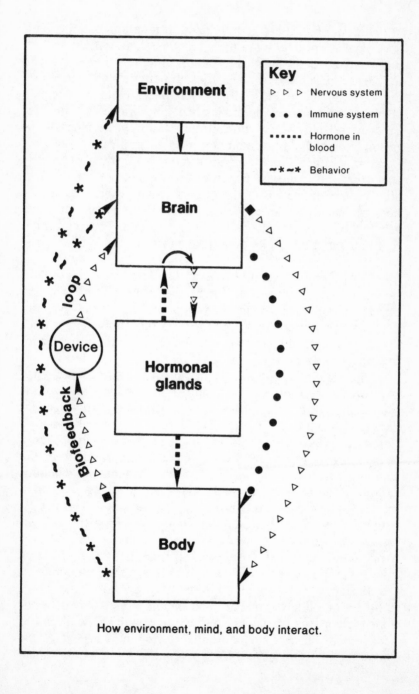

How environment, mind, and body interact.

as well, but often these go unnoticed. It monitors blood chemicals, oxygen level, temperature, and other signs, without intruding into your consciousness. For any number of reasons, you may want to gain control over these functions, and you can do this with the help of biofeedback technology. Note that the map shows a biofeedback loop linking body and brain. The "device" in the loop may be a sophisticated brain-wave monitor, or simply a hand-held thermometer used as an aid in controlling skin temperature. The idea is the same—to tell you about bodily states that you otherwise would be aware of only remotely, if at all. The device has only a temporary place in the map. That's because once you learn to control an inner state, you have established a new feedback loop between your body and mind that can function on its own. (For more on biofeedback, see chapter 5.)

The diagram is complicated, and so are the studies that try to come to grips with what it pictures, as their names suggest: psychoneuropharmacology, psychoneuroendocrinology, and psychoneuroimmunology. And the term that sums them all up? Dr. Reiser uses the mind-bending "psychopathology-psycho-logic-psychophysiological process."

But don't let terms get in your way. The diagram can help to explain many curiosities of emotion and behavior. It shows how our emotions influence the resistance of the body to disease. For example, a bullish, confident mood seems to rally the body's defenses. What this means in practical terms is that once a person learns to change his or her attitude, changes in the immune system will follow. There is evidence that our emotions influence the progress of cancers, allergic reactions, and asthma. In an issue of the *Journal of Psychosomatic Research*, psychologist Lydia Temoshok, Ph.D., of the University of California, San Francisco, says that cancer patients who "freely expressed feelings of anger and distress had more positive immune response than those who suppressed their emotions."

It doesn't take medical tests to prove that the mind influences the body. You can read people's thoughts and emotions in their faces, of course, and in their bodies as well. In her book on ways people can continue growing in later years, *Your Second Life* (Delacorte, 1979), psychologist Gay Gaer Luce,

Ph.D., says that the body's posture reveals an unseen *mental* posture. Her work with older people has taught her that tense jaws, hunched shoulders, and stooped backs are deformed not so much by physical wear and tear as by holding in emotions over the years. To invert a statement made a few pages earlier: As the mind goes, so goes the body. The two are in this game of life together, and your ability to keep them working as a team is a full-time challenge, one that involves everything you do. That's why this book on thinking better isn't simply a collection of brain-building puzzles and memory tricks. Your best thinking begins below the neck, because it is grounded in health—in a well-nourished, regularly exercised, relaxed body, one that supplies your brain with nutrients, oxygenated blood, and the stimuli that come from a variety of physical activities.

2

Foods for Thought

You are what you eat.

So goes the popular saying. And our midriffs offer graphic proof of the connection between diet and body. A variation on that saying might be, "You *think* what you eat," because foods have psychoactive powers. These powers are found not just in certain mushrooms and alcohol, but in the everyday ingredients of sandwiches, lasagna, and omelettes.

The mind-altering effects of foods are subtle, and because of that we tend to overlook them. Researchers are only now charting the mental shifts that follow a meal or an overnight fast. But once you learn to recognize your reactions to certain foods, you can consciously plan your menus and mealtimes to favor mental work—or to settle the mind for a nap, if that's your pleasure.

You may have noticed the mental lethargy that tends to set in after eating a large, starchy meal; carbohydrates have been found to indirectly raise levels of a brain chemical that retards the firing of neurons and promotes relaxation. That's fine if you plan on taking a snooze, but not if you're about to launch into a challenging textbook. A better meal for mental performance might favor protein over carbohydrates, according to studies with both schoolchildren and older adults.

A second diet-brain interaction is at work when you find yourself light-headed and unable to concentrate after skipping a meal. You are feeling the effect of a temporary case of hypoglycemia, or low blood sugar. The brain is highly susceptible to ups and downs in blood sugar. That's because even though it is the hungriest organ of the body, it is able to store very little fuel.

The effects of diet are subtle, and not everyone reacts in the same way to the nutritional pushes and pulls of a particular food. You'll have to heed your own experience. Be alert to times when your mind is particularly sharp (or sluggish), and note what was on your plate for the past meal or two. Just as athletes watch their diets for the sake of peak performance when training, you can learn to alter your diet for the sake of mental output.

Researchers have been surprised to find just how vulnerable the brain is to the nutritional peaks and valleys that are a part of anyone's day.

"It remains peculiar to me that the brain should have evolved in such a way that it is subject to having its function and chemistry depend on whether you had lunch and what you ate," remarks researcher Richard J. Wurtman, M.D., of MIT.

But such is the case, and each of us should eat accordingly. The brain is dependent on the blood for nutrients that are the building blocks of neurotransmitters. If these nutrients are in short supply, our thinking is altered in ways that could leave us emotionally unstable or, to say the least, at less than our intellectual best.

Your Sugar-Fueled Computer

Generations of parents have passed on to their children the importance of starting the day with a good breakfast. The wisdom behind this advice has a lot to do with glucose, better known as blood sugar.

When we go into the kitchen each morning, we are coming off a fast, as acknowledged by the term "breakfast." We've been away from the table long enough to significantly lower the level of glucose in the blood. Some people find they can start their day without first bumping up this glucose level, but most of us have learned that the folks were right—we'll work better if we take time to eat a good breakfast.

Within just a half-hour after a drop in the blood's glucose level, the brain will be noticeably affected. The brain burns two-thirds of the body's glucose, and it is highly dependent on the blood for a steady supply of this fuel, day and night. Its billions of electrical circuits are always turned on, whether or not we happen to be involved with a knotty problem. This could be explained by the fact that only a tiny fraction of the brain is employed by any single activity, even test taking. (In fact, sleep researchers have found that the brain is hungriest not when we're awake but during periods of rapid-eye-movement sleep, when we're dreaming.) Glucose generates the 20 or 25 watts of electricity needed to conduct the brain's electrical business; it also is harnessed to produce the transmitters that monitor these transactions.

The brain keeps very little glucose on tap. That's because glucose is stored as glycogen, a bulky substance for which the inflexible cranial vault has little room. So, if you skip a meal or two and your blood sugar is running low, your body turns to its glycogen storehouse, the liver. This organ is free to contract and expand up to 50 percent as its supplies of glycogen come and go. If our brains had to accommodate their own fuel, we'd probably walk away from a big meal with balloonlike heads.

The Ups and Downs of Sugar

Given its appetite for sugar from the blood, wouldn't the brain run best if we ate lots of sugary, starchy foods?

The answer is no. A diet high in sugar and refined carbohydrates can foul up the delicate mechanisms that the body employs to iron out extreme levels of sugar in the blood. Sugar is released from the liver when levels run low, and surplus sugar is withdrawn from the blood for storage. When you tamper with the balancing process by binging on sweets, the symptoms can range from mild physical and mental reactions to the chronic, sometimes severely debilitating symptoms of hypoglycemia (abnormally low blood sugar).

You can informally examine your own responses to sugar and refined foods, and then change your habits accordingly. You probably already have several habitual, perhaps unconscious means of elevating your blood sugar for a quick lift. Gulping down a candy bar on a hike is an obvious example, but others are less apparent. A cup of coffee, even without a grain of sugar or drop of cream, briefly boosts blood sugar by stimulating the flow of adrenaline, which in turn causes the liver and muscles to discharge glucose into the bloodstream. Many soft drinks, containing both sugar and caffeine, deliver a double wallop. So do mixed drinks; the alcohol triggers the release of glucose, and the sweet mixer supplies the sugar. (In fact, gin-and-tonics have been found to mimic the effects of hypoglycemia in subjects with normal blood sugar metabolism.) If you usually light up a cigarette when you have a cocktail, you're adding a *third* factor, because nicotine also liberates blood sugar. Small wonder that, in our society, people at social events may carry a drink in one hand and a cigarette in the other. Or that long after-dinner conversations are often fueled by sweet aperitifs, dessert, cigarettes, and coffee or tea. Many of us habitually prepare for mental work with one or more of these aids. For example, writers may find themselves sitting "blocked" at the typewriter if they are without their customary cigarette or snack or drink.

Now that you have an idea of how sugar can work to lift you up, you can monitor for yourself the letdown that sometimes follows if you're sensitive to sugar. Look for a negative reaction—perhaps lethargy, or an inability to concentrate—from one to three hours after eating, especially if you have had a meal high in sugars and refined, starchy foods.

If you're unusually predisposed to low blood sugar problems, symptoms may include headaches, tingling sensations, sweating, dizziness, palpitations, and a desire for sweet foods. You may want to undergo a glucose tolerance test to find out if you're hypoglycemic. Regardless of the severity of symptoms, most people can be helped through changes in diet and daily habits. To better maintain a constant level of blood sugar, you should choose protein foods (meat, eggs, cheese, nuts, tofu and other soybean products) over starchy and sweet foods (white bread and pasta, corn, potatoes, and dried fruit). Eat protein snacks between meals, rather than restricting yourself to two or three big feasts each day. Your body will still be able to manufacture sufficient glucose on such a diet, through a slower synthesis from protein and fats. Remember to eliminate or cut way down on caffeine, tobacco, and alcohol, because they liberate glucose into the bloodstream. Regular exercise also is important in a personal program to counteract low blood sugar. Studies have shown that physical exercise improves glucose tolerance, and generally lowers levels of glucose in the blood.

Psychoactive Foods

Glucose is only one item on the mind's menu. The brain requires other nutrients as well to make the neurotransmitters that regulate our thought processes.

Although the brain's business is conducted by tiny electrical leaps between nerve cells, this flow of electricity is either triggered or held back by neurotransmitters. And levels of neurotransmitters correspond to levels of certain essential amino acids that we ingest.

Studies demonstrate just how closely our behavior is tied to what we eat. As mentioned earlier in the chapter, an elevated level of one particular neurotransmitter simply makes us feel drowsy. Deficiencies of other brain chemicals can cause symptoms ranging from mental fogginess to severe mental disorders. Older people tend to have generally lower neurotransmitter levels, and this could be a cause of the forgetfulness and the depression that are increasingly apt to visit us later in life.

The following pages offer a brief guide to favoring your mind's work by what you put on your fork. Note that research in this area is recent and ongoing, and many food-brain interactions are not yet fully understood.

Tryptophan and Drowsiness

Have you noticed it's sometimes hard to do mental work after a big, starchy meal? Rather than tackle an intellectually

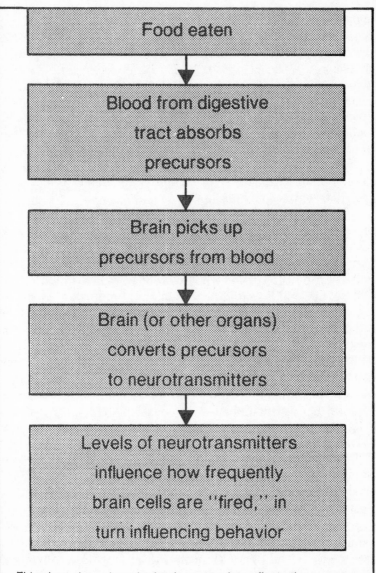

This chart shows how the food on your plate affects the way your brain works. The brain reflects the contents of a meal in a matter of minutes.

demanding task, you may be more inclined to drop into a comfortable armchair and nap. The popular explanation for this "siesta response" is that the blood has gone to the aid of your stomach, leaving your brain and the rest of your body in a state of lassitude.

But researchers have traced post-meal drowsiness to a neurotransmitter, called serotonin, that is indirectly supplemented by certain foods we eat. Serotonin subdues the electrical transmission between neurons, and can induce sleep. Small wonder that we find the mind is less than attentive after a big, starchy meal. The amount of serotonin generated from a meal can relieve occasional insomnia.

Tryptophan is the active ingredient in food from which the brain synthesizes serotonin. This amino acid is particularly plentiful in meat and dairy products, and you can consciously plan your meals and work hours so that you won't be drowsy at your desk, or full of ideas when your head is on the pillow.

So, the goal is to minimize serotonin production when you want to do mental work, and then to encourage its production in order to get a better night's sleep—and to be more productive the next day.

But there's a curious wrinkle in managing serotonin levels. Just because you eat lots of tryptophan doesn't mean you'll make more of it available to your brain for conversion to serotonin. That's because tryptophan-rich foods also happen to contain generous amounts of other amino acids, and these nutrients have to compete to enter the brain.

You might think the brain would welcome all the nutrients it could get. But it is one of the few organs (along with the eyes and the testes) that are selective about which substances they accept from the blood. Before it can enter the brain, a nutrient has to be ferried across what is called the blood-brain barrier—a natural screening mechanism which ensures that our minds aren't swayed by every toxin and drug that flows down the bloodstream. Tryptophan competes with its fellow amino acids for a ride from these carriers. You can increase its chances of admission to the brain by eating carbohydrates along with protein foods. Here's why: Carbohydrates cause the pancreas to secrete insulin, a hormone that encourages the skeletal muscles

Good Sources of Tryptophan

Food (100 g)	Tryptophan (mg)
Cheddar cheese	341
Peanuts (roasted)	340
Turkey (light meat, roasted)	340
Tuna (canned in oil, drained)	285
Tuna (canned in water, drained)	277
Chicken (roasted)	250
Beef (chuck)	217
Cottage cheese (4% fat)	179
Milk (skim)	49
Milk (whole)	49
Yogurt	20

Sources: Martha Louise Orr and Bernice K. Watt, *Amino Acid Contents of Food*, Home Economic Report No. 4 (Washington, D.C.: Agricultural Research Service, U.S. Department of Agriculture, 1968).
Consumer and Food and Economics Institute, *Composition of Foods: Dairy and Egg Products*, Agriculture Handbook No. 8-1 (Washington, D.C.: Agricultural Research Service, U.S. Department of Agriculture, 1976).
Consumer and Food and Economics Institute, *Composition of Foods: Poultry Products*, Agriculture Handbook No. 8-5 (Washington, D.C.: Science and Education Administration, U.S. Department of Agriculture, 1979).
Bernice K. Watt and Annabel L. Merrill, *Composition of Foods*, Agriculture Handbook No. 8 (Washington, D.C.: Agricultural Research Service, U.S. Department of Agriculture, 1975).

to pick up the other amino acids from the blood. That means more tryptophan can enter the brain and more serotonin is produced. You feel relaxed, drowsy, ready for bed.

That's why the Argonne National Laboratory recommends that if you're about to go on long, tiring flights, you should eat a high-carbohydrate dinner the night before departure (see Successfully Weathering Jet Lag and Swing Shifts, in chapter 3).

How should you go about planning a meal that will make

sleep come more easily? When Samuel Seltzer, D.D.S., of Philadelphia's Temple University School of Dentistry, experimented with the mind-altering effects of tryptophan (in this case, to decrease dental pain), he suggested subjects eat a low-protein meal of 10 percent protein, 10 percent fat, and 80 percent carbohydrate.

Incidentally, alcohol should not be part of that meal. If you're in the habit of having an alcoholic drink to settle you down for a good night's rest, you should know that alcohol has been found to cause the blood/brain barrier to allow less of certain amino acids into the brain, possibly restricting the production of neurotransmitters. Specifically, decreased levels of serotonin have been found in the brains of alcoholics who had committed suicide.

Tryptophan uptake by the brain is greatest two to four hours after eating a starchy meal. This could explain the custom in some countries of taking a siesta in the afternoon, when the daily tryptophan peak happens to coincide with the contribution made by lunch.

You can give in to the urge to nap each afternoon. But many of us need to keep on our mental toes throughout the afternoon. Studies suggest that you can stay more alert by laying off the carbohydrates at lunch and emphasizing protein instead. In one experiment, subjects over 40 years of age were found to be

---

Tryptophan in Pill Form

Dietary tryptophan is safe, even for those apt to be most sensitive to it—the elderly and people under stress. The nutrient can also be taken as a pill, but researchers caution that patients with liver disease and those on certain medications should not take tryptophan. In fact, everyone—whether they're undergoing medical treatment or not—should check with their doctor before using tryptophan in pill form.

especially prone to a mental lapse after a high-carbohydrate "lunch" of non-dairy sherbet. As reported in the *Journal of Psychiatric Research* (vol. 17, no. 2), they performed worse than people who consumed a protein meal of turkey in a test requiring sustained attention.

Similar effects have been noticed after breakfast, too. Kids are less sharp in school following a high-carbohydrate breakfast, according to C. Keith Conners, Ph.D., research professor of neurobiology at Children's Hospital National Medical Center in Washington, D.C. His studies found that mental performance is worse still if children eat something sugary along with the starchy food. (Dr. Conners's work is discussed later in this chapter.)

Again, protein can help keep the brain alert. Some studies suggest that for breakfast to carry you effectively through to lunch, it should serve up a full 15 grams of protein—about the amount in 2½ medium-sized eggs. Other good morning protein sources are blender drinks made with yogurt or cottage cheese plus milk, with fruit added for flavor.

Independently of your menu, your blood level of tryptophan varies on a daily cycle, typically hitting a peak a couple of hours on either side of lunchtime and reaching its lowest point between 2 and 5 A.M. But don't assume this means your brain will be at its perkiest between 2 and 5 in the morning, and that you'll be your best as a night owl. Tryptophan may be waning in the wee hours, true, but other vital signs (including levels of adrenaline in the brain) are also low at this period.

Clearly, then, the complex and mysterious brain can be lulled by something as mundane as a big plate of spaghetti. And recent studies have shown that its performance is affected in quite a different way by another amino acid, one that's found particularly in egg yolk, liver, and soybeans—choline.

Choline for Memory Function

A memory tonic has yet to hit the market. But one nutrient in the vitamin B complex, choline, has been identified as a key to memory function.

Like physical stamina or a flat stomach, our memory is a resource that we take for granted when young, then try to hold on to in later years. Forgetfulness is often made light of—the white-haired absent-minded professor is a stock character role—but to older people, memory loss isn't funny. The prospect of severe memory loss, whether it be a symptom of senility in general or Alzheimer's disease in particular, is enough to frighten anyone.

That's why choline has gotten so much attention from researchers. The fattest volume of the respected reference series *Nutrition and the Brain* (Raven Press, 1977) is devoted to the role of choline alone.

One of the volume's editors, John H. Growdon, M.D., of Tufts–New England Medical Center Hospital, writes that "preliminary studies on normal subjects and patients with Alzheimer's disease are extremely provocative. A large segment of society would benefit if it were found that lecithin [a soybean product high in choline] improves learning or memory in normal subjects or in patients with Alzheimer's disease, or makes people more efficient in other cognitive tasks or in motor

A "Think-Better" Formula?

You can buy nonprescription supplements that promise to maintain "thinking ability." One such formula contains lecithin (from which the body makes the neurotransmitter acetylcholine) and ribonucleic acid (RNA). RNA is a nucleic acid, molecules of which contain the genetic programming that guides the formation of all biological matter. The reasoning behind RNA in a think-better formula is that our genetic coding tends to break down in later years, and that it can be rejuvenated through oral supplements. But Dr. Hendler stresses in *The Complete Guide to Anti-Aging Nutrients* that he has found *no support* for claims that people can aid memory or learning by eating RNA supplements.

performance." Research continues, in hopes that serious mental decline can be reversed nutritionally. At the University of Ohio's Brain Aging and Neuronal Plasticity Research Group, director Ronald Mervis, Ph.D., calls their ongoing work with choline "very promising."

Choline is a nutrient that should be of interest to anyone valuing a vital mind. It has been credited with three major roles: It apparently increases the rate of the brain's metabolism; it is the substance from which the brain makes acetylcholine, a neurotransmitter involved in memory function; and it is thought to help maintain the structural integrity of the synapses, which are the points of communication between brain cells. Levels of choline characteristically drop as we age. And levels are particularly low in people with Alzheimer's disease, the most common form of senility. Alzheimer's has been linked to impairment of acetylcholine's function in the brain, among other possible causes, and choline has been used experimentally to halt the tragic loss of memory that accompanies the disease. When 11 patients with Alzheimer's took lecithin, 7 of them experienced a substantial improvement—50 to 200 percent—in long-term memory.

You don't have to be old or clinically senile to be eligible for choline's benefits. Younger people are also affected by choline levels. In one study with college students, choline supplements improved performance on memory tests. Another study showed that the memories of college students suffered when acetylcholine levels were artificially lowered by a drug; the students became forgetful, much as if they had aged prematurely.

Even for the great majority of older people who aren't troubled by senility, there is normally some decline in the effectiveness of acetylcholine. The reasons aren't known: The aging brain may be physically less able to use the neurotransmitter; certain chemicals in the brain that inactivate neurotransmitters may be doing too good a job; or the brain could be producing too little acetylcholine simply because the diet is deficient in choline-rich foods. Ohio State's Dr. Mervis suspects that choline can help to retard the effects of *normal* aging on the brain, from midlife on. He believes it would be especially prudent of those who have a parent with Alzheimer's to take a daily supplement.

These offspring have an estimated 40 percent greater chance of getting the disease themselves. "So," says Dr. Mervis, "they may want to do something preventive beginning in their thirties and forties rather than wait around for eventual signs of cognitive impairment." That's not to say choline has been proven to have protective powers—but until its roles are well established, a daily supplement over the years can be a safe and affordable form of nutritional insurance. A last-minute treatment with choline, on the other hand, can't bail out a person showing severe impairment, says Dr. Mervis. "The brain has already been ravaged, and you can't expect miracles." (Of course, you shouldn't take this or any supplement without your doctor's approval and supervision.)

Are most older people walking cases of lecithin deficiency? Dr. Wurtman, who is series editor of the five volumes of *Nutrition and the Brain*, believes that what is considered a "normal" level of lecithin in the diet may become insufficient as people age. He suggests that "choline or lecithin may even improve memory among otherwise normal young people with relatively poor memory functions."

Why would a standard diet fail to provide our brains with sufficient choline as we age? Because we're living so long now, suggests Dr. Mervis. He suspects that senility was much less of a problem in centuries past, because life spans were shorter.

Choline in Your Diet

How much choline is enough to keep your mental equipment working smoothly? And what are the best sources? Sheldon Saul Hendler, M.D., Ph.D., in his very readable book *The Complete Guide to Anti-Aging Nutrients* (Simon and Schuster, 1985), closes his review of lecithin by saying that the nutrient apparently plays significant roles in a number of intellectual functions, memory in particular, and he recommends including lecithin-rich foods in the diet, substituting cabbage and cauliflower for eggs if a person is particularly concerned about cholesterol. He neither recommends nor speaks ill of lecithin supplements, and suggests a top end of 1 gram of supplemental choline or 10 grams of lecithin per day. Take more, cautions Dr.

Good Sources of Choline

Food	Choline (mg)
2 large eggs	800
3 oz beef liver	578
1 tbs lecithin granules	250
3 oz fish	100
1,200 mg lecithin capsule	25

Source: U.S. Department of Agriculture Nutrient Data Research Group, 1981.

Hendler, and you risk nausea and vomiting, possible dizziness, and giving off a fishy aroma.

Some choline is synthesized by the liver, but most is supplied through the diet. The National Academy of Sciences says that a person typically gets from 400 to 900 milligrams of choline from the diet each day, but no Recommended Daily Allowance has been set. See the chart, for good sources of choline. If, with your doctor's approval, you decide to take a lecithin supplement, read the label carefully. Some types are better than others. In fact, the percentage of choline they contain varies from a low of 20 up to a high of 96. The useful form of choline is called phosphatidylcholine, or PC for short. The purer forms of PC aren't available to us as supplements; the stuff is a waxy compound which is quick to become rancid, and storage is difficult even in the laboratory. Dr. Mervis says that one company may release a choline product unusually high in PC in response to his encouraging findings, but he puts the maximum practical proportion of PC in an over-the-counter product at about 60 percent.

The more choline you have in your diet, the higher the levels that are available to your brain. That's because choline, unlike tryptophan, has its own carrier in the bloodstream and doesn't have to compete for passage across the blood-brain barrier.

What, then, is the bottom line on choline and mental performance? Choline has promise as a key to preventing serious senility in the later decades of life. And it may well have a much more universal benefit, says Dr. Mervis, as a preventive that can be enlisted by the "80 percent of us who will remain basically normal but might otherwise experience mild cognitive impairment. We know that all animals, including humans, show some degree of memory loss with aging. What looks exciting as far as man is concerned is prevention."

Vitamins and Minerals for Peak Mental Performance

"Dietary inadequacy of any one of the vitamins could be expected to alter brain metabolism," writes G. Harvey Anderson, M.D., and Janice L. Johnston, M.D., in the *Canadian Journal of Physiology and Pharmacology* (March, 1983). And yet the best nutritional mix for the brain is still unknown. The effect of even relatively common vitamin deficiencies remains "virtually unexplored," the authors say.

Up to this point, researchers have focused their work on the mental deficits caused by extreme deficiencies of nutrients. As important as this work is, those of us who are reasonably prudent about what we eat are left without a nutritional plan to follow for peak mental performance. Dr. Anderson and Dr. Johnston, who are on the faculty of medicine at the University of Toronto, point out that only since the 1970s have researchers begun to look into the mental impact of a "normal" diet, with its daily variation in ingredients and quantity and the occasional skipped meal.

The following pages review the latest practical information available on nutrition and the brain. We'll start with vitamins.

The B Vitamins

The B vitamins work in the body to help convert proteins, carbohydrates, and fats into fuel, and in the brain to help synthesize mood-controlling chemicals. That's why a B-vitamin deficiency often manifests itself in extreme muscle weakness and in psychiatric problems ranging from mild irritability to full-blown psychosis. Fortunately, severe cases are rare, but even a marginal deficiency can leave you with the blues and the blahs.

For example, a marginal deficiency of *thiamine* (vitamin B₁) may make itself known through a feeling of lassitude. Vitamin B₁ is needed to produce and use one of the brain's major chemical messengers, acetylcholine, says Gary E. Gibson, Ph.D., a thiamine researcher at the Cornell-Burke Rehabilitation Hospital in White Plains, New York.

Insufficient *niacin* (vitamin B₃) may cause such symptoms as depression, emotional instability, and loss of recent memory, according to Anderson and Johnston in the *Canadian Journal of Physiology and Pharmacology*, and that's "well before any physical evidence is present." A severe deficiency of niacin is known as pellagra.

It's rare that a person gets insufficient *vitamin B₆*, or pyridoxine, but a deficiency may result nevertheless, for a couple of reasons. A person may have higher-than-average requirements (as in the case of infection or chronic disease); and B₆ may interact with certain drugs, including hydrazine, the artificial coloring tartrazine (or FD&C Yellow No. 5), birth control pills, and PCBs (a group of toxic chemicals that have found their way into the environment).

Vitamin B₆ is involved in the production of two chemical transmitters in the brain, dopamine and serotonin. It is plentiful in meat, fish, bran cereal, watermelon, and bananas; but it is also found in a wide range of foods. Some 20 to 30 percent may be lost through cooking.

A lack of vitamin B₆ has been associated with depression, hyperactivity, autism, and schizophrenia. When French researchers supplemented the diets of autistic children with B₆ and magnesium, the children improved. Instead of withdrawing from activity, they were more interested in people and events and better able to communicate. They also had better patterns of sleeping and eating.

Deficiencies of *vitamin B₁₂* have been associated with a range of mental effects: psychosis, numbness, severe memory loss, and confusion. A deficiency may cause the brain and spinal cord to degenerate. Less dramatically, a low intake of B_{12} has been linked with the impaired production of the neurotransmitter acetylcholine. Researchers at the University of New Mexico School of Medicine found that people age 60 or older with even a mild B_{12} deficiency had impairment of their memories and abstract thinking skills. Low blood levels of B_{12} are common enough among hospitalized psychiatric patients that routine testing for the nutrient has been recommended.

In his survey of the medical literature, Dutch physician Cees J. M. van Tiggelen has found further indications that vitamin B_{12} plays a role in memory function. A deficiency of this nutrient may cause the brain to use less glucose and synthesize less acetylcholine. A brain low in the neurotransmitter nor-adrenaline may pick up less B_{12} through the blood-brain barrier. And exposure to toxic chemicals also may prevent people from taking full advantage of the B_{12} in their diets; apparently, mercury, heavy metals, and certain solvents prevent the transfer of the vitamin from the blood to the brain.

Pernicious anemia is the disease caused by a lack of B_{12}. It is caused when the body's failure to produce digestive acids, or stomach surgery, prevents the vitamin from being absorbed from the diet. A vitamin B_{12} deficiency can also be caused by certain medications, including Aldomet, Slow-K, neomycin, and para-aminosalicylic acid. People who eat no meat, fish, or dairy products are at risk, because B_{12} is the one vitamin not present in plant foods. Sheldon Saul Hendler, M.D., recommends that vegans (who eat no animal products of any kind) be alert to signs of a deficiency—nervous disorders such as weakness in the limbs—and that they take a general supplement.

Vitamin B_{12} supplements are not a cure-all for the mental blahs, although Siegfried Kra, M.D., writes in Aging Myths that the nutrient "used to be a cherished, fashionable form of treatment by the old-time physicians for persons complaining of weakness or numbness, depression, anxiety, or memory loss." But Dr. Kra, a professor at the Yale University School of Medicine, does not recommend B_{12} injections unless a patient has a proven insufficiency.

How does a doctor know when to check for a deficiency? "Severe mental disorders usually begin when people are in their twenties," explains Frederick Goggans, M.D., who is director of the neuropsychiatric evaluation unit at the Psychiatric Institute of Fort Worth. "So when an older person comes into the hospital with mental problems and has no prior history of a mental disorder, I'm sure to screen for B_{12} deficiency.

"Depression and dementia in the elderly are the two syndromes most classically associated with B_{12} deficiency," Dr. Goggans says. "Dementia closely resembles senility, with its loss of intellectual function. But when it's caused by B_{12} deficiency, it's reversible." Unfortunately, some elderly people may be written off as senile when their condition is actually treatable.

"Biochemical depression is also very common in the elderly," adds Todd Estroff, M.D., assistant director of neuropsychiatric evaluation at Fair Oaks Hospital in Summit, New Jersey. "They're especially susceptible because they don't eat well. The older person with poor teeth who tries to survive on tea and toast is more likely to develop a deficiency."

One study of 49 patients in the geriatric psychiatry unit of a Massachusetts hospital found B_{12} deficiency more than any other undiagnosed medical problem (*Journal of the American Geriatrics Society*, December, 1982). In another study, published by three doctors from Denmark, low values of B_{12} were found in one out of every three patients admitted to a geriatric center (*Acta Medica Scandinavica*, vol. 200, no. 4).

Folate (or folic acid) is a B vitamin that is found plentifully in leafy greens; its name is taken from the Latin word for "leaf," *folium*. Folic acid can be broken down by cooking food sources at high temperatures, points out Venezuelan researcher Luis A. Ordsnez in *Nutrition and the Brain*, volume 1 (Raven Press, 1977). And normal cooking temperatures of 110°C to 120°C (230°F to 250°F), over a period of just 10 minutes, can destroy up to 65 percent of this nutrient. A deficiency of folic acid has been found to cause irritability and forgetfulness. Together with B_{12}, it plays a role in the brain's production of acetylcholine. According to researchers writing on vitamins and the nervous system in *Nutrition and the Brain*, volume 3 (Raven Press, 1977), up to 30 percent of psychiatric patient admissions may be deficient; and they cite one study in which 67 percent of the patients admitted to a psychogeriatric ward were found to be deficient in folate.

A folate deficiency can come about either through poor nutrition or an inability to absorb the nutrient. Drugs that have been found to block the uptake of folic acid include Aldomet, Bactrim, isoniazid, neomycin, methotrexate, Epanutin Capsules, Dyazide, and Premarin.

Vitamin C

The body has found dozens of ways to employ *vitamin C* (ascorbic acid). In the brain, it plays a part in the conversion of one neurotransmitter, dopamine, to another, norepinephrine. Vitamin C is an ingredient in the complex recipe for the two chemical messengers that are part of our survival instinct: the hormone adrenaline and the neurotransmitter norepinephrine. They stimulate our "fight-or-flight" response to danger, and a deficiency of C can cause mental sluggishness. Vitamin C also plays an important supporting role, helping the body to pick up more of another nutrient particularly important to brain function, iron. Vitamin C can best perform this iron-boosting function if it is taken with meals.

In spite of our great need for vitamin C, our bodies are unable to produce it. Most plants and animals can; but we, along with apes, guinea pigs, and fruit-eating bats, must get our vitamin C through our diets.

It could be that our appetites for vitamin C-rich foods are controlled by the brain. Fruits and vegetables may become more attractive to us when the cellular electrical potential drops in brain cells low in vitamin C. If this theory is true, it means that our appetites are governed by a neurological feedback mechanism that helps us eat as we should.

Vitamin E

Recent work by Finnish doctors suggests the potential of *vitamin E* and another antioxidant, *selenium*, to treat senility. The study, by Matti Tolonen, M.D., of the University of Helsinki, was presented to researchers from around the world who gathered for a conference in China.

For a year, 15 residents of a Finnish nursing home took 600 international units of vitamin E daily, plus selenium. Another 15 received placebos (fake pills). Neither the participants nor the supervising nurses knew which patients were getting the vitamins. After only two months, some people had improved so much mentally and emotionally that the nurses said they could easily guess who was getting the vitamins. At Dr. Tolonen's request, they wrote down their guesses. The nurses were correct 80 percent of the time.

What they noticed, and psychological evaluations backed up, was that the elderly residents taking the vitamins were more alert, open to change, willing to care for themselves, and interested in their environment. They were less depressed, anxious, hostile, and tired. And while many mood- and mind-altering drugs have as many bad as good effects, this treatment had *no* adverse effects, Dr. Tolonen reports.

Trace Elements

Trace elements are vital to the mind as well. Of the hundred-odd elements on this planet, roughly one-quarter find some use in the human body, and most of these are classified as trace elements. As the term suggests, very little of each trace element is found in the body—less than 1/100 of a percent of the body's weight. And each trace element makes up at most only a matter of a few parts per million in our diet. Still, without these minute contributions of mineral matter from the soil and sea, we could not live. The essential trace elements include chromium, copper, fluorine, iodine, iron, nickel, silicon, tin, and zinc. Then there are the ultratrace elements, which take part in biological reactions but for which no deficiencies have been described as yet; they include arsenic, barium, bromine, cadmium, and strontium. Finally, some elements are regularly found in animal tissues but may be present simply as contaminants from the outside world. A few of the many elements in this category are gold, lead, mercury, silicon, silver, and titanium.

If you think some of these sound poisonous, you're partly right. Any trace element can become toxic if enough is ingested. As E. J. Underwood explains in *Trace Elements in Human and Animal Nutrition* (Academic Press, 1971), an element has a sequence of effects on the body as more and more is ingested. At an optimal level, the element functions biologically, as a *nutrient*; at a higher dosage, the element works pharmacologically, or in other words as a *drug*; take still more, and the element becomes a *toxin*, and may cause illness or even death. In general, Underwood says, "concentrations must be maintained within narrow limits if the functional and structural integrity of the tissues is to be safeguarded."

A number of trace elements have a direct effect on the mind's work, and research in this area is attracting more attention. For example, at the USDA's Grand Forks Human Nutrition Research Center in North Dakota, research psychologist James Penland, Ph.D., is investigating marginal or subclinical deficiencies among adults. He is looking into the effects that may only show up under stress, in situations that demand a lot of a person's resources. He hopes to find out how nutrition can help a person to achieve "optimal behavior," that is, to perform better with less effort.

Dr. Penland's work clearly is a departure from the nutritional science that deals with malnutrition and glaring omissions in the diet. In time, he says, we can expect to see new RDAs (Recommended Daily Allowances) established for more of the trace and ultratrace elements. To date, he says, the investigation of subclinical deficiencies "has really been neglected," but he believes that situation will change.

Here is a brief survey of the effects of some important trace elements on brain function. This will not be the last word, and you can expect to hear news of other effects as studies currently in progress begin to bear fruit.

Iron for Anemic Intellects

The brain requires a great deal of oxygen if it is to function effectively, and dietary iron plays a vital role in getting it there via the blood.

Specifically, oxygen is carried by hemoglobin, the red protein that gives our blood its color. If our diet is low in iron, both the production and function of hemoglobin are impaired. The symptoms of an oxygen-starved brain include lowered alertness, a shortened attention span, and trouble learning new material. Boosting iron intake may reverse these problems. Anemic infants have been made more alert and responsive after only a week of oral iron supplements. In adults, one study established a correlation between blood iron levels and fluency with words; volunteers were asked to come up with as many words beginning with "Q" and ending with "L" as they could, and higher iron levels were associated with a greater number of words.

Iron is also thought to play another important cerebral role, as a component of several neurotransmitters, including serotonin, dopamine, and noradrenaline.

Iron may play a role in schizophrenia through its influence on dopamine levels in the brain. Researcher Don M. Tucker, Ph.D., suggests that drugs used to treat this mental disease may work by altering the way iron is transported in the brain.

Curiously, iron has been found to affect one half of the brain more than the other. The brain's halves, known as hemispheres, may look like mirror images, but they have different functions. Now, researchers at Grand Forks have found that the nutrient is particularly important to the left brain hemisphere of right-handed people. What's more, men and women respond differently to iron supplements.

Sixty-nine college students, all right-handed, were involved in the study. Their blood was measured for its iron level, and they were given six tests of mental ability. In one, they were asked to list words beginning with "Q" and ending with "L." Another task measured their ability to remember a series of audible tones. The Grand Forks researchers found that the higher the iron level in the students' blood, the greater was their word fluency—which in right-handed people is a left-brain function. The researchers did not find the same kind of connection between iron levels and ability to remember tones, which happens to be the right brain's department.

Further studies have shown that a daily ferrous sulfate supplement of 100 milligrams, in tablet form, brought about improved cognitive abilities in women subjects but did not affect the men. Dr. Penland believes that women are helped because they tend to be deficient in iron. The greater the deficiency, the greater the benefit; that's why response to the supplement varies with where a woman is in her menstrual cycle.

Dr. Penland says that the study will now focus on a group considered especially apt to benefit from iron supplements, female athletes. Because their physical activity uses up iron, they are more likely to be deficient in iron than are less-active women.

In what ways can iron sharpen thinking? Verbal fluency improves: That's the ability measured by tests of how many words a person can name in a 20-second period that begin and end with certain letters. Dr. Penland also observes that subjects can better sustain attention and readiness. Finally, optimal iron levels seem to help bring about an elevated mood state. Says Dr. Penland, "I would imagine, given the role iron plays in carrying oxygen, we might also see an increase in activity or vigor."

Iron deficiency is a prime suspect when a physician is confronted with a senile patient. Says Yale University School of Medicine professor Siegfried Kra, M.D., the patient's blood should be checked for low iron; if anemia is confirmed, the standard remedy is to administer iron tablets plus vitamin C to enhance absorption of the mineral. (This should be done only under the supervision of a doctor, of course.)

Are you getting enough iron to suit your brain? That depends a lot on who you are. Most men get an adequate amount if their diets are reasonably well balanced. Premenopausal women may not, and have a special need during pregnancy, labor, delivery, and lactation. Reflecting these differences, the RDA of iron is 10 milligrams for men, and 18 for women 50 and under (but 30 to 60 milligrams for pregnant and lactating women, and just 10 milligrams for women 51 and older). Many women may be well below these figures, according to a 1974 survey by the Department of Health, Education and Welfare. They found that 95 percent of women between the ages of 18 and 44 were receiving barely *half* the RDA of 18 milligrams. Dieters and the elderly are also at risk, simply because they are eating less. So are vegetarians, because iron is most plentiful in meats and fish. Vegetarians can choose from a wide selection of foods relatively rich in iron, however, including blackstrap molasses, lima beans, soybeans, sunflower seeds, spinach, and broccoli.

Iron absorption can be blocked in a number of ways—by antacids, tea, phosphate additives in food and beverages, several medications (tetracyclines, Aldomet, Premarin, and Theo-Dur), and the preservative E385. Absorption can be dramatically *enhanced*, on the other hand, if a vitamin C-rich food is eaten along with the iron source.

The Role of Zinc

The body's need for iron tends to overshadow its dependence on another mineral, *zinc*. And according to the *Medical Tribune* (September, 1983), many diets consumed in the Western world do not supply enough zinc. "Since zinc is present in relatively high concentration only in meats and seafoods, it is likely that a large portion of the population may have only a marginally adequate intake of zinc," says the report.

And the impact on the zinc-deprived brain? Effects are seen most often in older people, but are by no means restricted to them. Symptoms may include mental lethargy and apathy, and may be traced to the neurotransmitters dopamine and norepinephrine. Zinc may also affect areas of the brain that receive and process information from taste and smell sensors. This has led researchers to investigate zinc's role in eating disorders such as anorexia and bulimia. Researchers at the University of Colorado Health Sciences Center, in Denver, report that underweight boys whose dietary zinc was deficient responded well to zinc supplementation of 5 milligrams twice a day. After one year, the boys had increased their daily intake of calories by almost 50 percent (*American Journal of Diseases of Children*, March, 1984).

Zinc may also play a role in senility. A hospital study in the United Kingdom found that blood zinc levels among 220 demented patients were significantly lower than those of nonsenile patients. A possible cause is zinc's influence on the work of neurotransmitters in the brain. British researcher Roy Hullin, M.D., found low zinc levels among a younger group of patients (under 65) who were just starting to show signs of senility.

The elderly may not be getting an adequate supply because many can't afford the foods (such as meats and seafoods) that are high in this nutrient. Dr. Hullin says there's a "strong case" for more work in this area and possibly for "zinc supplementation to the population at risk."

A Smart Diet for Kids

Your brain never outgrows its need for a good diet, but the nutritional demands of children are especially important if they are to reach their full intellectual potential. As Ralph E. Minear, M.D., Ph.D., advises in The Brain Food Diet for Children (Bobbs-Merrill, 1984), "From the time your child is born until he reaches his sixth birthday, what you feed him can be decisive in terms of his brain growth." In 1983, Boston University president Dr. John R. Silber stated that improved nutrition for pregnant mothers and the very young is crucial to "preserving the nation's intelligence."

Poor nutrition saps a child's IQ, independent of the effects of home life. That was the finding of Janina R. Galler, M.D., of Boston University School of Medicine. She and her colleagues reported in the Journal of the American Academy of Child Psychiatry (January, 1983) that malnourished children in Barbados score an average of 12 points lower on IQ tests than adequately nourished children in similar social conditions.

Dr. Minear, an instructor in pediatrics at Harvard Medical School, stresses the enormous value of breast-feeding for a child's development, because of both good nutrition and the psychological benefit of bonding between mother and infant. He suggests that breast-feeding continue for at least four to six months and up to a year or two. Mother's milk is "the single best brain food we know about," he says. And although a child must eventually leave the breast for solid food, Dr. Minear recommends a diet that continues to yield roughly the same ratios of nutrients as mother's milk: 50 percent fats, 35 to 45 percent complex carbohydrates (as provided by vegetables, fruits, and whole grains), and 8 to 15 percent protein.

Don't worry that your child's IQ will wither if you don't stock the kitchen cabinets with special brain foods. Minear stresses the *balance* of nutrients, spread over four or five small meals a day (to make up for the young child's small stomach), rather than advocating particular foods; in fact, one meal in his book's sample menus consists solely of ice cream with fruit syrup and a cookie. The path to genius should be so delectable!

Many parents pass on to their children what they themselves learned as kids years ago: that breakfast helps to start off the day right. C. Keith Conners, Ph.D., of Children's Hospital National Medical Center, in Washington, D.C., agrees with this popular wisdom. His review of the medical literature, going back to 1931, suggests that breakfast will improve a child's performance in school. In a study from the early 1950s, boys "had a definitely better attitude and a better scholastic record during the period when breakfast was included in the daily dietary regimen than when it was omitted." A review by Kenneth Pollitt and others in 1978 concluded that breakfast "may both benefit the student emotionally and enhance his/her capacity to work on school-type tasks" (*American Journal of Public Health*). Conners recommends that further studies look at food and blood sugar as if they were drugs, that they focus not only on behavioral changes, but also on altered ways of processing information in the brain. For now, it can be said that breakfast skipping "may not be critical" for kids who are doing well in school, but those who are already working to their capacity could be seriously affected.

Ernesto Pollitt, Ph.D., of the University of Texas School of Public Health, and co-workers set out to assess the effects of skipping breakfast on the problem-solving performance of healthy, well-nourished 9- to 11-year-olds. Each child was served breakfast between 8:00 and 8:30 A.M., then given a problem-solving test in the late morning. When the same procedure was later repeated after the kids had skipped breakfast, the researchers found that the children's problem-solving ability was significantly poorer. And levels of insulin and glucose in the children's blood were lower as well.

According to the researchers, "these findings support observations that the timing and nutrient composition of meals have acute and demonstrable effects on behavior." They theorize that "glucose and insulin changes ... may have a direct effect on levels of [chemicals] in the brain involved in cognitive function" (*Journal of Psychiatric Research*, vol. 17, no. 2, 1982/ 1983). Breakfast is apt to provide certain nutrients that may be scant in other meals, report Annette B. Natow and Jo-Ann Heslin in *No-Nonsense Nutrition for Kids* (McGraw-Hill, 1985). The vitamin C in fruit juice is particularly likely to be missed. If your children skip breakfast because they worry about gaining weight, you might pass on to them the curious finding that obese teenagers miss breakfast more frequently than do those with normal weights.

Large doses of vitamins have been used to treat learning disorders, with mixed results. In a study reported in the *Journal of Nutrition* (vol. 109, 1979), 20 learning-disabled children in the Toronto area showed no significant improvement when given high levels of four vitamins that researchers had previously recommended as effective. But interestingly, the sugar-free, low-carbohydrate diet accompanying the vitamin treatment was found to benefit 18 of the 20 subjects. Children who are already struggling in school may not only be endangered by what's *missing* from the diet, but also by what's all too plentiful— namely, sugar and refined carbohydrates.

The Hyperactive Child

An estimated 5 percent of primary schoolchildren are labeled as hyperactive—that is, troubled by any of a wide range of learning disorders and behavioral problems that make them difficult to handle in the classroom and at home. What's more, they aren't learning as well as they should, jeopardizing their chances for a productive adult life. Researchers and parents alike have speculated that a prime cause of hyperactivity is a child's reaction to certain constituents in the diet.

In the 1970s, the late Ben F. Feingold, M.D., was the first to focus the blame on diet. A pediatrician and allergist, Dr. Feingold became widely known for his belief that hyperactivity and learning disabilities can usually be traced to children's inherited reaction to things they eat. The so-called Feingold diet advocates omitting foods containing added colors, flavorings, and other additives, as well as foods containing salicylates, a group of compounds found in aspirin and occurring as a natural component of such foods as apples, oranges, grapes, tomatoes, and tea. (Dr. Feingold later excluded the additives E320 and E321. If you are travelling abroad he advises that you avoid monotertiary butyl hydroxylquinone also. All are antioxidants added to some foods.) If the child's condition is caused by a reaction to these substances, Dr. Feingold believed, then this "elimination diet" should produce a noticeable improvement within a matter of several weeks, or sooner in younger children. Then, to identify the guilty elements of the diet, foods should be reintroduced slowly, one by one, taking note of the child's reactions.

Dr. Feingold reported that the diet would help or cure one-half to three-quarters of those children troubled by hyperactivity and learning disabilities; specifically, he listed a "dramatic" improvement in scholastic achievement as a specific benefit. But his claims have spawned much debate among parents, pediatricians, teachers, and psychologists. Results of relatively informal experiments, in which parents evaluate changes in their children's behavior, may be impressive. But when the diet is studied in a more scientific manner, the claims made for it appear to be overstated; that is, improvements in behavior that impress parents may not be noticed in the classroom by teachers. This leads some critics of the diet to suspect that the placebo effect is at work here: Parents *expect* their children to be helped by the stringent diet. Further, the psychological tensions which may aggravate hyperactivity are likely to be eased when the whole family joins the child in selecting and preparing the approved foods.

In 1982, when the National Institutes of Health formed its Consensus Development Conference to study hyperactivity, the group was not able to endorse a policy of removing additives to relieve the condition. And in 1983, *Clinical Psychology Review* (vol. 3, 1983) surveyed 12 studies on the effects of food additives on hyperactivity and learning disabilities. In the article, Steven A. Waksman of Lewis and Clark College's department of counseling psychology concludes that "the data do not support the hypothesis that hyperactivity is strongly linked to artificial food additives." Only some 5 to 10 percent of hyperactive children may in fact be affected by food additives, he says.

In the past few years, debate over the Feingold diet and

hyperactivity has subsided in volume, but the issue has not gone away. If anything, it appears more complex than ever. Hyperactivity is widely recognized now as a group of some 80 behavioral problems and learning disabilities. The tendency is inherited, but it is also brought out by such problems as difficult pregnancies, traumatic childbirth, viral infection, psychological stress, or poor nutrition. And even if a change in diet *can* work, the strict regimen can be extraordinarily challenging for a family.

"It's difficult to oversee food intake in an impulsive youngster who's already difficult to control," says Michael Cohen, M.D., of the department of pediatrics at the University of Arizona. "And it's difficult to comply with the Feingold diet—it takes tremendous resources and discipline. And it's expensive." Dr. Cohen, too, mentions the placebo effect: "When it does work, you have to consider that expectation is part of the improvement. Many hyperactive children have been treated shabbily. So they tend to improve if they perceive a new optimism in people's attitudes toward them."

Still, some people continue to believe that the diet works miracles. The Feingold Association of the United States, a parent support group headquartered in Alexandria, Virginia, estimates that they've helped 100,000 families since the 1970s. They credit their success to a few key factors:

● The association provides families with a detailed list of offending grocery items by brand name.
● They provide families and their doctors with a list of medications that will not violate the Feingold diet.
● They enlist the help of pediatricians, psychologists, and teachers to deal with the causes of hyperactive behavior that go beyond diet.

Can sugar influence childhood behavior? Dr. Feingold said no. Many parents say yes. Most doctors aren't sure. Dr. Cohen remarks that "no scientific studies support the link between sugar and hyperactivity. But I see a lot of kids, 25 to 30 percent I'd say, improve after cutting out sugar. So why not try it?"

Dr. Feingold didn't believe that hyperactivity could be traced to non-food allergies, either, but again there is disagreement. Some doctors believe any food that can trigger classic allergic reactions—for instance, asthma—is equally capable of triggering hyperactivity. So if a child doesn't improve on the Feingold diet, it's worthwhile to check for allergies to dust, pollen, milk, or other common allergens.

What if neither diet nor psychological support helps your child? Stimulant drugs seem to calm kids down long enough for them to learn and get along with others. But many parents are uneasy about putting their young children on stimulants.

"Parents *should* be uneasy about drug treatment," says Dr. Cohen. "I would be, too." The children do become easier to handle, but at a cost: Their learning ability is not enhanced, and may even be further impaired. And the side effects of these drugs may include loss of appetite, sleeplessness, headache, stomachache, nausea, depression, even high blood pressure. Children should be monitored closely if drug treatment is necessary. Ultimately medication can't spare the hyperactive child from going on to experiencing problems in adulthood, including low self-esteem and a sense of failure.

Dr. Cohen stresses that the first course of action against hyperactivity should be a thorough diagnosis, followed by a team approach to treatment that includes special education, counseling, parental support, behavior-modification techniques, and nutritional treatment. Medication can help to facilitate those attempts but should never be the primary treatment, he believes. Pat Palmer, secretary of the Feingold Association, says basically the same thing. "If all other physical causes of hyperactivity have been ruled out, the Feingold diet is the next step. Drugs are a last resort."

So after analyzing the apparent controversy surrounding the Feingold diet, it appears that advocates and critics of the program aren't very far apart, after all. Both sides acknowledge the possibility that factors other than diet play an enormous and decisive role and cannot be ignored. Both acknowledge that the diet is difficult but not impossible to follow. And both agree that drugs are a last resort and should be used with caution.

What should you do if you think your child is hyperactive? First, have your child evaluated to find out if he or she is truly hyperactive and if there is a physical or psychological cause. Ask your family doctor or pediatrician for advice. If no one can determine the cause, the Feingold diet may be worth a try.

"I think it's fair to state that the Feingold diet may help a small number of younger children," says Bernard Berman, M.D., associate clinical professor of pediatrics at Tufts University School of Medicine and chief of pediatric allergy at St. Elizabeth's Hospital in Boston. "If all medical causes have been ruled out, it's okay to try the Feingold diet for a couple of weeks." That seems to be a very short time. But Dr. Berman adds, "What's the sense of continuing to restrict a child's diet—with all the social implications of making a child feel different, giving him or her special cookies and so on—if it doesn't seem to be doing any good?"

Dr. Berman sums up the issue neatly by saying, "There's no quick fix. If a child is truly hyperactive, the best bet is to get help from a good health-care group—skilled people who are trained to chart a course of action for your child."

Special Needs in Later Years

Most of the work on the mental effects of diet have dealt with school-age children, despite the fact that learning ability and alertness are important at every stage of life. You can teach an old dog new tricks, especially if that dog has had an adequate diet.

But studies on diet and aging have largely steered clear of mental powers, and concentrate instead on physical symptoms. That's in part due to the attitudes of our society, researchers included. We tend to regard senility (the mental component of aging) as inevitable, and therefore beyond the help of something so straightforward as diet. The truth is, however, that most of us can look forward to keeping our wits well into old age; and many apparent victims of senility are actually suffering from other health problems that, once identified, can be reversed. Poor diet is one of them.

Another reason researchers may be reluctant to study the influence of nutrition on mental status is the sensationalism surrounding extravagant claims popularly made for this or that vitamin therapy.

A third reason is that it's a challenge for researchers to tell the difference between the several causes of brain dysfunction in older people: Poor nutrition can produce the same mental symptoms as heart failure, thyroid disease, or toxicity from medication.

Of those few studies that do deal with this area, almost all have concentrated on institutionalized elderly people with serious problems. What of the great majority of older Americans who go about their lives normally? Recent surveys suggest that up to 50 percent of them may in fact be getting less than the RDAs of essential nutrients.

Researchers at the University of New Mexico School of Medicine decided to study this forgotten group. James S. Goodwin, M.D., Jean M. Goodwin, M.D., M.P.H., and Philip J. Garry, Ph.D., tested the hypothesis that the gradual decline in certain mental functions commonly associated with aging is brought on at least in part by "subclinical" deficiencies, a nutrient intake that doesn't cause disease but may contribute to lots of other problems. For their study, they gathered 260 healthy older people, ranging from 60 to 95 years of age, who were well educated, financially well-off, and living independently. Their dietary intakes and blood levels of key nutrients were noted, and these levels were correlated to their scores on two tests of cognitive function: the Wechsler Memory Test, and a gauge of abstract thinking and problem solving ability called the Halstead-Reitan Categories Test.

The results, printed in the *Journal of the American Medical Association* (June 3, 1983), confirmed the hypothesis: Subclinical deficiencies are related to mental deficits, even among older people in excellent health. Specifically, the researchers found "an association between poor performance on cognitive tests and low intake and serum levels of riboflavin, folate, vitamin B_{12}, and ascorbate [vitamin C]." (The paper does mention the outside possibility that cognitive impairment leads to a poor diet, rather than the other way around.) Dr. James Goodwin concluded, "I think that to be on the safe side, anyone over 65 should take a multivitamin. They eat less—people over 65 are eating only about 70 percent as much as they used to—and therefore they're going to be getting less nutrients."

So, what you eat can have a lot to do with keeping your mind sharp in later years. But eating right can become a challenge, for a number of reasons.

First, our dietary needs change as we age, and yet you won't find these changes reflected in the RDAs. That's because RDAs are calculated from data on younger people. Older people are left to decide for themselves (ideally, with the help of their physicians) just which nutrients should be bolstered.

People do tend to modify their diets over the decades, but often for the wrong reasons. "Many older people eat an astonishingly small amount of food," reported the Ten-State Nutrition Survey undertaken by the U.S. Department of Health, Education and Welfare in the early 1970s. They may exclude hard-to-chew meats, an excellent source of protein and many nutrients, because of lost teeth or ill-fitting dentures. Instead, they are apt to favor soft, overcooked foods, which tend to be shy on micronutrients, especially minerals and the water-soluble vitamins. Other factors that work to impoverish the diet in later years include disease, prescription drugs, and alcohol, any of which can dampen appetites or impair digestion.

As for the food that is selected, it may be only partially digested because of decreased secretion of digestive acids and pepsin. The toll could be the less efficient absorption of iron, calcium, vitamin B_{12}, folic acid, and protein. Further along the digestive tract, aging intestines may not manage to pick up sufficient calcium to compensate for an older person's increased need for that nutrient.

Also important to keeping the mind vital in later years is ensuring that the brain continues to get a good supply of well-oxygenated blood. With this as their goal, researchers at the Longevity Research Institute in Santa Barbara, California, came up with a diet that they thought would increase the supply of oxygen to the brain. The menus were high in complex carbohydrates (representing 80 percent of total calories) and fiber, and low in protein and oils. Meals contained little meat, and no added refined sugars or salt. The 31 subjects in the study, all of whom had histories of some cardiovascular disease, were given no supplemental vitamins; smoking and drinking alcoholic and caffeine beverages were forbidden.

The results? The researchers noted that the most-changed scales on the California Psychological Inventory included "verbally fluent; quick, clear thinking; intellectually able; efficient; and perceptive." They conclude that a fatty diet slows down circulation in capillaries to the brain, and that a low-fat diet, in league with exercise, can deliver well-oxygenated blood to the brain and "enhance cerebral functioning."

How many cases of mental cloudiness in older adults can be traced to nutritional problems? Dr. James Goodwin says that these cases are the minority. But whatever the percentage may be, he believes "it is tragic to miss the ones you could help" through improved nutrition.

3

No Mind Is an Island

This chapter describes the subtle ways in which your environment influences your mind's performance. The brain is a highly sensitive instrument. But unlike a computer of the electronic kind, it can't be tucked away in a climate-controlled room or sturdy plastic case.

Your brain goes where you go, to noisy offices and polluted cities, through time zones and sudden climate changes. And as you might guess, it works better in a friendly environment than in a stressful one. Fortunately, you can go a long way toward making your surroundings more conducive to clear thinking.

It's curious that these mental stresses tend to be by-products of the very conveniences we would find it hard to live without. The automobile creates noise and airborne pollutants. Similarly, the background din of a television can interfere with reading and relaxation. Even narrow-spectrum artificial lighting may be harming our environment. Some particularly sensitive people may find that their work suffers in the short days of winter because they aren't getting enough bright, full-spectrum light. Such people "should become more attentive to their environment," advises Norman E. Rosenthal, M.D., a psychiatrist researching this syndrome at the National Institute of Mental

Health. He has found that even a slight sensitivity to light may keep people from working at their full potential when days are short.

Few of us would go so far as to blame a lack of full-spectrum light for a lousy day at the office. But one researcher, Albert Paul Krueger, M.D., LL.D., notes the "modern trend which recognizes that living forms react to seemingly minor environmental inputs, chemical and physical" (*Immunology and Allergy Practice*, July/August, 1982). These subtle inputs include even air ions, notes Dr. Krueger. He reports that air-conditioning and forced-air systems strip the indoor atmosphere of these electronically charged particles which are thought to promote mental alertness and freshness.

It seems that our minds are jarred by many aspects of technology that we simply haven't grown accustomed to—windowless offices, fluorescent lighting, highly processed foods, pollutants in air and water, the background roar of highway and industry, and the godlike ability of jet travel to stretch and contract the 24-hour day.

So, the challenge is to be stimulated by our busy world without letting it wear us down. This chapter suggests how to do just that.

Sound Advice

Of all the brain-numbing forms of stress and pollution, which is the toughest to exclude from your life? Noise, most likely. In an environment dominated by machines and crowded with people, a little sonic privacy can be hard to find. Noise slips over office partitions and under locked doors, travels easily through glass, and has driven some lovers of quiet to the ultimate in sound-deadening walls—sheets of lead. You can expect the din to get worse, according to projections by the Environmental Protection Agency.

The physical harm caused by loud noise is widely acknowledged today, and legislation now protects us somewhat from noise in the workplace, on highways, and at airports. But only recently have researchers and government regulators become

Prevent Ear Abuse

Your brain takes much of its information from two holes in the sides of your head—your ears. Although the trip is short, messages may be muffled and garbled in later years. When conversation, lectures and sermons, meetings, music, and the audio portion of movies and television are hard to hear, life is impoverished; hearing impairment isolates people, and makes them tentative in unfamiliar situations.

But are old ears necessarily poorly functioning ears? To answer this question, doctors from four countries traveled to a remote area of the Sudan of Africa, hoping to test the hypothesis that a virtually noise-free environment could preserve hearing ability well into old age. Their story was told in the *Annals of Otology, Rhinology, and Laryngology* (vol. 71, 1962). The researchers, visiting the country in the early 1960s, found a culture living at a late Stone Age level of development. Until a few years before, no other cultures had penetrated the area, and the technological noisemakers of the West were unknown. Even drums were not used.

The results? The tests confirmed that *noise* wears down our ears, not time. The society's elders had near-perfect hearing.

concerned with the effects of noise on the mind. Addressing a Senate subcommittee, Jack C. Westman, M.D., professor of psychiatry at the University of Wisconsin, has said that noise can impair both emotional well-being and productivity through its action on the nervous system. The effects of noise run deep. Even though you might become acclimated to a noisy environment, your body continues to react to the stress as animal bodies have for eons—as if the sound announced danger. Here's what happens next: Adrenaline is released into your bloodstream; breathing and heartbeat quicken; blood pressure goes up; and pores release sweat. And how does this translate into the work you do? Noise not only can reduce the *amount* of work you can get done, but is apt to drag down the *quality* as well. Intellectual tasks are especially vulnerable to noise.

So it is that, if you can find a way to dampen the din, you may experience a broader focus of attention, plus improved memory and recall. Your moods may lighten, too, so that you feel more inclined to get involved with life.

Music to Think By

There's also evidence that certain sounds can help us feel better and work more efficiently. A succession of beautiful, rich sounds is known as music, of course. Even plants are said to respond positively to it. In one study, plants exposed to classical East Indian music actually wrapped themselves around the speakers, while rock music *killed* other plants.

Whether or not you buy these stories, you can prove for yourself that humans are definitely susceptible to music. When you're not preoccupied with something else, play several different types of music—rock, jazz, fast classical, slow classical— and be alert to any effects on your mind or body.

Music can facilitate mental work at two levels, says Steven Halpern, Ph.D., a West Coast composer who has studied the effects of music on the mind. Most commonly, he says, we use music "in the background as a sound conditioner which blankets some disturbing noises." Any form of music can perform this simple function, but most have the drawback of attracting attention to themselves—even placid classical pieces.

People assume that classical music, because it isn't driven by a loud and simple beat, must be ideal background music for studying or other mental work. But that's not necessarily so, according to Dr. Halpern. He finds that classical pieces are beautiful, yes, but so beguiling that they can be distracting. And pop songs tend to be worse. They have tension built in, Halpern explains. The chord progression and melody of a tune work to generate in the listener a need for resolution—and this is the musical payoff known in the trade as the "hook," the part of the song that makes you want to hear it time and again. For this reason, most commercial music won't allow the mind to rest.

Dr. Halpern goes deeper in his discussion of why rock and mental wholeness don't go together. He says that the basic rock-and-roll back beat—an "anapestic" short-short-long, pause—"is unhealthy because it opposes the natural beat of the heart and is contrary to the rhythm of the arterial pulsations." As a result, he says, this music can confuse the body's own rhythms. And in the brain, theory has it, the two hemispheres lose touch. The toll is perceptual handicaps, stress, poorer performance, errors, and inefficiency. Furthermore, rock is addictive, says Dr. Halpern, and you may have to kick the habit by taking a vacation from this music.

In America, Dr. Halpern produces tapes of music that leave out the hooks, the chord progressions, and the heavy beat. "So," he says, "you're not hung up waiting for the next musical phrase." And yet, it isn't the characterless mood music that's piped into hotels and supermarkets. If Dr. Halpern's music is without the usual earmarks, then just what is there to it?

One cassette consists of piano or electric keyboards played with a great deal of "sustain," so that the individual notes blend together. At times, songbirds can be heard in the background. And occasionally a barely audible voice utters indistinct words— Dr. Halpern's messages addressed to the subconscious mind.

Dr. Halpern began making tapes with affirmations for his own use in the 1970s. He believes that his type of music prepares the mind for absorbing information easily, so that the spoken messages slip in effortlessly. "We can enhance creativity by speaking directly to the subconscious," he says. Motivation may be bumped up a notch, too, he found from studies with schoolchildren. "They enjoy their classes all of a sudden, and they don't know why."

Learning to Music

Background music is used to make learning come easier in a method pioneered by Bulgarian researcher and psychiatrist Dr. Georgi Lozanov. In foreign language courses and language

Music to Learn By

Here are the selections that researchers have used to put language students in a learning frame of mind. The "A" pieces accompany a slow and solemn reading of the material; the "B" pieces a normal speaking voice.

1. (A) J. Haydn, Symphony no. 67 in F Major, and no. 69 in B Major. (B) A. Corelli, Concerti Grossi, opp. 4, 10, 11, 12.

2. (A) J. Haydn, Concerto for Violin and String Orchestra no. 1 in C Major, and no. 2 in G Major. (B) J. S. Bach, Symphony in C Major, and Symphony in D Major; J. C. Bach, Symphony in G Minor op. 6, no. 6; W. F. Bach, Symphony in D Minor; C. P. E. Bach, Symphony no. 1 for String Orchestra.

3. (A) W. A. Mozart, Haffner Symphony, Prague Symphony, German Dances. (B) G. F. Handel, Concerto for Organ and Orchestra, J. S. Bach, Choral Prelude in A Major, and Prelude and Fugue in G Minor.

4. (A) W. A. Mozart, Concerto for Violin and Orchestra, Concerto no. 7 in D Major. (B) J. S. Bach, Fantasy in G Major, Fantasy in C Minor and Trio in D Minor, Canonic Variations and Toccata.

5. (A) L. V. Beethoven, Concerto in E-flat Major for Piano and Orchestra, op. 73, no. 5. (B) A. Vivaldi, Five Concerti for Flute and Chamber Orchestra.

6. (A) L. V. Beethoven, Concerto for Violin and Orchestra in D Major. (B) A. Corelli, Concerti Grossi, op. 6, nos. 3, 5, 8, 9.

7. (A) P. I. Tchaikovsky, Concerto no. 1 in B-flat Minor for Piano and Orchestra. (B) G. F. Handel, *The Water Music.*

8. (A) J. Brahms, Concerto for Violin and Orchestra in D Major, op. 77. (B) F. Couperin, "Le Parnesse et l'Astree," Sonata in G Minor, J. P. Rameau, Pieces de Clavecin, nos. 1, 5.

9. (A) F. Chopin, Waltzes. (B) G. F. Handel, Concerti Grossi, op. 3, nos. 1, 2, 3, 5.

10. (A) W. A. Mozart, Concerto for Piano and Orchestra no. 18 in B-flat Major. (B) A. Vivaldi, *The Four Seasons.*

Source: Reprinted by permission from Georgi Lozanov, *Suggestology and Outlines of Suggestopedy* (Gordon and Breach, 1978).

tapes, the material is recited in a rhythm that suits the particular classical piece being played. During the first repetition students follow along in their textbooks. The second time through, they close the books and simply listen as the teacher reads. (See the box, Music to Learn By, for a list of compositions that have been found to be particularly effective in these foreign language programs.)

The music seems to work by placing people in what Dr. Lozanov calls the "concert state," in which they are physically passive but mentally alert. (Other ways to arrive at the same state include biofeedback, relaxation exercises, and yoga.)

When we are in the concert state, learning becomes a relaxed process, rather than an exercise in cramming facts into an unreceptive brain. On one Italian language tape, for example, menu items are recited every several seconds over a track of soothing classical music.

This "suggestopedic system," as it is called, is intended to take advantage of the enormous influence on our minds of suggestion—that is, information that we absorb without necessarily being aware of it. Advertisements use the power of suggestion; so do successful orators and psychotherapists. We are continually picking up cues from our environment.

As evidence of the effectiveness of suggestopedic learning, Dr. Lozanov mentions adult language students who have learned 1,000 words in a single session. And he cites studies suggesting that the percentage of words memorized remains surprisingly constant with increasing age. Lozanov-method foreign language courses are available now in America. The musical pieces listed in the box, Music to learn By on page 52, were found to heighten learning of a language in Dr. Lozanov's researches.

The Pursuit of Quiet

Despite the fact that mental work often thrives on peace and quiet, we tend to resign ourselves to noise, to regard it as an inevitable price to pay for our advanced technology. Many of us retreat to our homes to escape the din, but households generate their own sonic pollution: the noise produced by vent fans, garbage disposals, blenders, and arguing, energetic kids—often to the accompaniment of a television in the background.

But you don't have to let noise invade your ears. You can plan your acoustic surroundings, just as you pick out comfortable furniture and pleasing colors for the walls. Here are some ways to improve your sonic environment, starting with your ears themselves.

Plug Your Ears

When you can't unplug a noise source, consider plugging your ears. You have several alternatives. The first choice is between devices that fit in the ears (earplugs), those that block the outside of the ear canal (canal caps), and acoustic earmuffs.

Make a Sound Check

You don't have to be aware of sounds for them to jam your mental channels. So, if you're going to track down sound pollutants in the environment, you have to be still and listen carefully. "Take a sound inventory," says Steven Halpern. Write down all the sounds you can hear—music, talking, traffic, and even unidentifiable tapping and whirring—and put a check mark by any that you find pleasant or mentally stimulating. Once you have your list, you can proceed to act on dampening the unpleasant sounds and taking advantage of the helpful ones, as this chapter shows how.

Earplugs are the most popular of these. They are small, unobtrusive, and relatively comfortable. Although earmuffs keep out more noise, plugs should lower sound levels to the point that they aren't likely to challenge your powers of concentration. You can count on them to shave off roughly 13 to 15 decibels (db) in the low frequencies and some 25 to 30 db in the high frequencies. Three types of earplugs are available. *Premolded* plugs come already shaped to suit the average ear, and some brands are sized. These plugs are meant to be reused. More accommodating to the individual shape of the ear are *formable earplugs*, which are pliant enough to conform to the ear canal. They are used only once. And *custom-molded* earplugs are fitted by a trained person. Understandably, custom-molded plugs cost more than the other types, but they are highly effective and typically last longer.

As simple as they are, earplugs are not without their potential problems, and the following tips can go a long way towards making them more comfortable and effective.

- Earplugs tend to loosen when the jaw moves in laughing, talking, and chewing; and people tend to pull at them and loosen them in warm weather and when the plugs have

---

Racket Ratings

In America, The Environmental Protection Agency has estimated that nearly half of the population is regularly exposed to noise levels capable of interfering with health. And remember, it's not only the quantity of sound that drives you wild, but also the way in which you perceive it. Some housing sites have been disqualified for federal financing because crickets chirping in the neighborhood have exceeded the government's noise levels—and yet few people would find this natural sound to be offensive. Curiously, a near-total silence can be uncomfortable. A typical response of visitors to a sound-proofed chamber is to compulsively turn around to see what may be lurking behind them.

Sound	Decibel Level
Dripping tap	40
Moderate rainfall	40
Refrigerator	45
Chirping birds	60
Washing machine	65
Kitchen mixer	70
Vacuum cleaner	70–75

continued

Cocktail party (100 guests)	70–85
Busy traffic	75–85
Alarm clock	80
Diesel truck	80
Window air conditioner	80
Electric shaver (at close range)	85
Screaming child	90–115
Live rock music (amplified)	90–130
Chain saw	100
Pneumatic drill	100
Motorcycles	100
Tube train (inside)	100
Power mower	100–105
Football crowd	120
Loud thunder	120
Jet engine (at takeoff)	120–140
Air-raid siren	130

been in place a long time. But plugs should fit snugly in order to do their job well.

- If premolded plugs are causing you discomfort, your ear canals may be of an unusual shape. Consider switching to custom-molded plugs, or earmuffs.
- Other causes of discomfort are infection and allergic response to the plug material. Either case may warrant a shift to earmuffs.
- Earplugs don't last forever. Heat, humidity, and earwax all take their toll. Check them from time to time to see if they have shrunk or hardened.
- Reusable plugs should be kept clean by regular washing.

Some people use a Walkman-type personal stereo with headphones to block out a noisy world. But Maxwell Abramson, M.D., of the department of otolaryngology at Columbia University School of Medicine, cautions that the music may mask the acoustic environment so effectively that a person becomes unaware of sounds that would otherwise serve as warning signals—the rush of an oncoming car, for example, or the beeping of a smoke alarm.

White Noise

Instead of cutting down on the noise, you may find it easier to cover it up with "white noise." This is a bland, background sound that doesn't call attention to itself and yet has the ability to mask noises that set you on edge. You can buy either a mechanical white noise generator (it spins to create a pleasant whirr) or an electronic one that employs a speaker.

But you don't have to invest in a generator. A similar effect can be had simply by tuning a radio between stations and adjusting bass and treble controls for the best noise-muting hiss. You can produce a soothing sound remarkably like falling rain. Even a fan or air conditioner on a fast setting can mask unpleasant sound with a sound that quickly becomes an innocuous part of the background.

In the Home and Office

You can make your workspace or quiet room at home less vulnerable to sounds, and you don't have to truck in lead walls.

And If You Don't Want to Hear a Pin Drop . . .

Here are some more radical steps for creating an oasis of quiet. To block the sound of traffic, the neighbor's dog, and other outdoor noises, you can supplement the windows of your quiet room with heavy sheets of store-window glass. It is available from local glass suppliers; for ease and safety of handling the heavy glass, have the shop grind the edges. Make sure that you caulk around the new panes, just as you would to exclude cold winter air. To block noise coming from within the building, you can install a tight-

continued

fitting, solid-wood door (modern hollow-core doors are acoustically quite transparent) or go so far as to erect a second layer of thick drywall along interior walls. If the floor is transmitting an unacceptable level of noise, you can even lay down a new wood floor on top of the existing floor. In mansions built a hundred years ago, when money was less of an object, floorboards were sometimes actually laid over a layer of sound-deadening sand!

As a rule, dense materials like wood, wallboard, and glass do the best job of *stopping* noise, while porous materials (like carpet) can help by *absorbing* noise.

That's an important difference, and one that many people find confusing. Won't a curtain block noise? "It's not going to do a bit of good," says acoustics engineer Dean McAdoo of Noise Unlimited in Somerville, New Jersey. "Not unless it has vinyl behind it and it seals around the edges of the window." Acoustical tile doesn't block noise either. Rather, "it only keeps down the reverberating sounds generated within the room." And carpet? "You're much better off using acoustical tile on the ceiling than you are laying a carpet on the floor," McAdoo says. A thin indoor-outdoor carpet is especially ineffective at absorbing sound, but a deep-pile carpet will do a better job.

If you still can't quite believe that curtains and floor coverings allow most of the sound to pass right through, here's a simple experiment that will convince your ears. Simply place a piece of either material over a card table so that it drapes to the floor, crawl under, and listen. You'll find that sounds may be muffled somewhat but they aren't much diminished in volume.

Doors and windows are two ways of plugging a room so that less noise gets in. A solid wood door will exclude noise better than a hollow, lightweight one. Even in summer, close shutters if you have them (and if you're not dependent on a cool, fresh breeze to make the room livable). Should you be considering the decision to blow insulation into the exterior walls of your house, a benefit you may not have thought of is that you'll also gain some insulation from the sounds entering your home from the neighborhood. A row of trees or shrubs bordering your lawn may give you visual privacy, but Dean McAdoo says that they do little to reduce sound. The principal benefit of a green barrier is psychological: If a noise source is out of sight, it may be out of mind as well.

Another noise-fighting strategy is simply to generate less of it. Today's home tends to be a cacophonous castle, with an average background noise level of up to 60 db. Here are some tips for achieving some peace and quiet in your home:

- Place foam pads, like those sold for typewriters, under kitchen appliances that turn countertops into sounding boards. Similarly, you can place a noisy refrigerator on a square of carpet.
- To prevent dishwashers and washing machines from rattling the plumbing, have them installed with flexible connections.
- When shopping for an appliance, typewriter, or printer, look for a quiet model. (Remember, it may sound quieter in a noisy store than it would at home.) Plastic covers are an inexpensive way to quiet a typewriter or printer.
- In many homes, televisions and radios are kept on throughout the day even though no one is watching or listening. Turn them off to cut down on background noise. Or, keep headphones handy to preserve the peace.
- Fluorescent lights consume less electricity than do incandescent bulbs, but they may hum in an annoying way. Consider switching to an incandescent (screw-in bulb) fixture.
- If your loved ones are the source of the din, establish a quiet hour—a daily period in which each family member is free to do as he or she pleases so long as it doesn't generate very much sound. You may find that everyone welcomes a ritual time set aside for quiet conversation, reading, studying, drawing, or writing letters.

Is Sunlight an Essential Nutrient?

Artists appreciate the powers of light. In fact, Henri Matisse was afraid that the all-out colors of his brilliant Fauvist canvases might actually blind him. He described color as a "savage and gluttonous god."

Matisse wasn't talking that way because the turpentine fumes had gotten to him. He intuited years ago what researchers are just now learning in the laboratory—that light somehow reaches into the brain and stimulates our thoughts and emotions. Today, the biobehavioral power of light (that is, its ability to affect our behavior by affecting our brains) is a lively area of research. Studies reveal that our bodies need to be exposed to full-spectrum light—not just the few parts of the spectrum radiated by most lamps—if we are to feel energetic and to perform at our best. Researchers in the Soviet Union have been so impressed by the ability of light to lower people's reaction times and improve their performance at work and in school that full-spectrum lighting has been installed in many of the country's buildings. In Norway there's a law that every employee is to receive a certain amount of natural lighting. And in U.S. and Canadian schools, supplementary full-spectrum lighting has been credited with reducing absenteeism and decreasing hyperactivity among first-graders.

Why is it that we seem to need a daily ration of light? Consider that life on this planet evolved under a powerful, full-spectrum light source, the sun. Its invisible infra-red rays warm the air and soil. Plants use the blue and red rays to power photosynthesis. In animals, changing light levels may be the cue that causes them to prepare for winter.

When ultraviolet (or UV) light falls on humans, it enables the skin to synthesize vitamin D; and blue light is the most effective color for preventing jaundice, a condition that can cause brain damage in infants. Now, researchers are probing the dramatic effects of light on human behavior. Specifically, mood and performance suffer when a person's doses of light are either too little or too irregular—a quite recent problem in our history on Earth, dating from when we humans moved indoors. Most of us work inside. Our leisure hours are probably spent under a roof, too. What little sunlight does reach us may be filtered through a blanket of polluted air, and then again through window glass and glasses or sunglasses. Typical indoor lighting can do little to supplement our impoverished light diet; neither incandescent nor fluorescent lights are biologically active because they are too dim and offer too little of the spectrum.

The *timing* of our light doses is important, too. That's why sunrise and sunset have an influence on human behavior. Workers on night shift or swing shift may miss both of these celestial events, with ill effects similar to those experienced by travelers who fly across several time zones—their patterns of sleep, eating, and hormonal and neutrotransmitter release may all be thrown off, a syndrome known to travelers as "jet lag." (For tips on reorienting yourself, see page 72.)

We vary greatly in our sensitivity to light. Symptoms of a deficiency range from simple lethargy and off-days at work to suicidal depression. But the effects are real enough that Alfred Lewy, M.D., Ph.D., and his associates at Oregon Health Sciences University refer to light as a "drug," one that can be used to treat certain types of depression and sleep disorders (*Psychopharmacology Bulletin*, vol. 19, no. 3, 1983).

Winter Doldrums and the Third Eye

The mechanisms by which light works these surprising effects aren't fully understood. But the investigation has led to a site deep within the head—the pineal gland, which happens to be the "third eye" that reads light levels in certain other animals.

Don't Blame It on the Moon

The word "lunacy" has its root in the Latin word for moon. Indeed, the moon has been blamed for a psychiatric wardful of mental disorders, including pyromania, suicide, homicide, alcoholism, lycanthropy (turning into a werewolf), and sleepwalking, as well as for loss of reason.

But a survey of the medical literature absolves the
continued

moon of guilt, according to an article in *Psychological Bulletin* (vol. 85, no. 5, 1978). David E. Campbell and John L. Beets of the University of Kansas found little reliable evidence to support the moon's international reputation as an influence on our minds. They reviewed studies of admissions to psychiatric wards, calls for counseling assistance at a college campus, and the behavior of patients under psychiatric care.

The researchers suggest that people should stop blaming mental distress on the moon, and turn their attention instead to the "unexplored frontier of environmental psychology," including the effects of temperature, turbulence, air ion concentrations, seasonal changes, and even the earth's magnetic and cosmic rays.

The pineal releases melatonin, a hormone that travels in the blood to trigger changes throughout the mind and body. Specifically, melatonin helps to regulate our daily and seasonal rhythms. The lower the light, the more melatonin is secreted. The short days of winter cause elevated levels of this hormone, and a substantial number of people respond much as a bear does when hibernation time approaches—they crave carbohydrates and put on weight, sleep longer hours, and avoid social contact. But instead of crawling off to the nearest cave, human sufferers of this problem (known as Seasonal Affective Disorder, or SAD) become less efficient, lose energy, and contract a host of symptoms that can loosely be described as "the blues."

At the National Institute of Mental Health in Bethesda, Maryland, staff psychiatrist and researcher Norman E. Rosenthal, M.D., tested the hypothesis that winter blues might be reversed by exposure to light—bright, full-spectrum light, administered both before dawn and after dusk in order to create what the brain would perceive as a spring day.

Dr. Rosenthal placed an ad in a local newspaper to solicit victims of winter blues and was impressed by how many people responded. At this early stage in his research, he can't estimate what percentage of us are affected by SAD; but he says there must be "a great number," to judge by the many people who have come to him with the telltale symptoms: an annual depression that comes on in the autumn and departs in the spring.

As you might suspect of a disorder connected with the sun, the farther north you go, the stingier the sunlight and the worse the depression. Symptoms are relieved by traveling south. This is the experience of pathologist Gary Hill, M.D. As a Texan, Dr. Hill was untroubled by winter blues until he moved to Baltimore. His symptoms were aggravated when he moved north again, to Philadelphia. He has found that clouds and smog may further reduce the natural light that finds its way into the eyes. On a trip to San Francisco, Dr. Hill was brought down emotionally by the foggy skies over the city even though it was summer.

Supplementing Your Light Diet

"People susceptible to SAD should become sensitive to their environment," advises Dr. Rosenthal. They need to introduce more light into each day to suppress melatonin secretion, but standard levels of light at the office or home probably won't do the trick. In working with SAD victims, Dr. Rosenthal and colleagues have used a light box containing eight 40-watt, full-spectrum fluorescant lamps. Phillips manufacture such a lamp, called the Graphica tube, although a standard fluorescent fixture with two tubes would serve well enough.

Dr. Gary Hill has his own light box, but he doesn't lug it along when he travels. Instead, he makes do with the lighting available in his lodging. Arising before dawn, he turns on all the lights in the bathroom and reads there until the sun comes up. To be effective, conventional lighting must be three to four times its usual intensity.

But you don't need bright lights to accomplish what the sun does naturally. Daylight is a free and bountiful resource. According to neuroendocrinologist Richard J. Wurtman, M.D., the simplest way to send messages to your pineal gland is to make the most of winter's meager sunlight: Get out of doors early and late in the day and open curtains to let the sunshine flood in. Melatonin levels go down, and spirits and performance go up. Steve Miller, an associate of Dr. Alfred Lewy, says, "even the cloudiest day here in Portland provides far more than the lights used experimentally."

Miller emphasizes that the important factor is the apparent length of the day—the timing of the onset and offset of light. Consequently, people whose work (or personal habits) causes them to miss dawn or dusk or both are experiencing artificially shortened daylight periods, so that they go without the biological cues which regulate their internal clocks. Later in this chapter, you'll find ways to adapt to work shifts and long-distance travel.

Choosing the Right Light

Of course, light serves a far more obvious function, as well. It enables us to see what's in front of our faces. But we tend to underestimate the level of light needed to perform at our best. An article in the *Lancet* (March 24, 1979) relates a British study of older blind people in which half were discovered to be visually disabled by poor lighting.

We need to be increasingly aware of the quality and quantity of light as we age. That's because the cornea and liquid within the eye become cloudy, the retina grows less responsive, and the muscles that focus the iris are less fit. A simple antidote for these problems, according to the *British Medical Journal* (June 23, 1979), is to increase the intensity of the light source by bringing it closer to the work. For example, by moving the light from 8 feet away to 4 feet, you quadruple the amount of light falling on your work.

The Light Debate: Tube versus Bulb

Fluorescent tubes are in wide use in offices, factories, and schools because they create roughly four times more illumination than an incandescent bulb of the same wattage. Tubes put off less heat, too, which can be an important consideration in summer.

continued

But fluorescent lighting isn't without its drawbacks, some more solidly substantiated than others. Some people complain of skin reactions to the light, headaches, and fatigue; others are concerned about the ultraviolet radiation certain tubes give off (a plastic shield will both absorb most of these rays and also diffuse the light to cut down on glare).

And some people just don't like the way they *feel* sitting under banks of fluorescents. The light may seem too bright, too cool in color, too flickery, or too noisy. The respective remedies for these problems include relying more on individually controlled task lighting; switching to warmer-looking bulbs; changing worn-out tubes or starters and admitting daylight into the room; and replacing ballasts that hum with quieter units.

The best level of illumination varies from situation to situation. Jeanne Stellman, Ph.D., and Mary Sue Henifin, M.P.H., write in *Office Work Can Be Hazardous to Your Health* (Pantheon, 1983) that you don't need as much light to navigate a hallway as you do for work at a desk. And at a desk, the optimal light level goes up as the size of the details you're working with goes down. The tiny items involved in drafting demand a higher-than-standard light level, for example. You should also shed relatively more light on visually demanding work, such as deciphering messy writing, and on work that has to be done quickly.

To adjust light levels to suit the job, you are best off with an individual lamp that supplements overhead fixtures. Lamps on adjustable arms further allow you to customize your lighting as needed. Stellman and Henifin also recommend that indirect lighting (which bounces off a wall or ceiling) should provide one-third of the illumination, with the other two-thirds coming from a direct source such as a desktop lamp. Ideally, your workplace should be bathed in both natural and artificial light, for the sake of both accurate color perception and the emotional lift that daylight seems to give.

A great lighting system won't do you much good if it bounces light off the work or desktop right into your face. You can remedy most problems by diffusing the light from bulbs with translucent shields and fluorescent tubes with translucent panels. You can't clip a shield over the sun, of course, so the answer lies in a window shade. No matter what the light source, it should come from the side or from behind you, never from in front. And you can use a blotter to cut the glare from a shiny desktop.

If you spend much time looking at the video screen of a personal computer, your work may go more smoothly if the room has indirect lighting. That's the conclusion of a study in the illumination laboratory at the University of Colorado, summarized in *Corporate Design and Realty* (January/February, 1985). Forty-eight subjects worked in an office setting, performing a task on a personal computer with a video monitor. The subjects were asked to evaluate lighting systems: Indirect lighting was provided by fluorescent bulbs that diffused light throughout the room; and the direct source consisted of fluorescent tubes mounted in conventional ceiling fixtures.

The indirect lighting system won on several scores, both objective and subjective. It produced less glare on the screen; created a more pleasant working environment; made the subjects feel more productive; and was picked three-to-one over the direct lighting system, even though both the systems in the study provided sufficient illumination for the task.

A room with a view may help bring out your best, as well. The visual quality of your surroundings can affect the amplitude of your brain waves, according to Roger Ulrich, Ph.D., of the University of Delaware. Working in Sweden, he studied the influence of both urban and bucolic settings on viewers. He discovered that when people view natural settings with vegetation or water, their alpha wave levels are higher than when they look upon an urban environment devoid of plant life. (Alpha brain waves are associated with an alert, yet relaxed state of mind.) Dr. Ulrich sees this as strong evidence that views dominated by nature are better able to elicit the wakeful, relaxed state and can help us stay alert for longer periods. However, Dr.

Ulrich points out that this doesn't mean we will be more *productive* in such a setting; problem-solving activity is associated with the beta-wave state, which may carry with it feelings of stress.

You may have heard that color can influence the mind. Dr. Ulrich mentions the "pink room effect," in which a certain warm hue of paint is supposed to benefit mental work. "That just seems to be mysticism at this point," says Dr. Ulrich. But he acknowledges that, "in very general terms, color studies seem to suggest that certain colors, such as blue and green, tend to reduce arousal. If you're excited, these colors tend to be calming, whereas colors such as oranges and reds tend to activate, or increase arousal." But even these broad conclusions have to be tempered with the fact that your reaction depends a lot on the particular shade and intensity of the color.

Ultimately, says Dr. Ulrich, "there are no hard-and-fast rules of thumb about the effects of room colors on people." The particular shade that delights you and seems to best suit your mind may not work for someone else. So, rather than rely on a universally beneficial shade, you have to experimentally visit rooms to find how they feel to you. As the journal *Architectural Technology* (Spring, 1985) concludes in an article on lighting systems, "In the absence of scientific guidance, architects can trust human beings to know what makes them feel good."

Witches' Winds and Ion Generators

At the offices of a large British insurance company, medical researchers installed experimental equipment that manipulated the quality of the interior atmosphere for more than a hundred employees. With the equipment turned on, workers reported fewer headaches and significantly improved alertness, freshness, and comfort.

The machines that caused this welcome change were air ion generators. The year was 1981, and the reputation of air ion research was on the rebound from a severe debunking at the hands of the scientific community in general and, in America, by the FDA in particular. Until the American government squelched them in the early 1960s, advertisements for negative ion generators had made rather extravagant claims of healthful benefits. This overselling of the generators set back serious research on air ions, writes Albert Paul Krueger, M.D., LL.D., in the journal *Immunology and Allergy Practice* (September/October, 1982). A veteran researcher in the field, Dr. Krueger is heartened to observe "that air ion research, both basic and applied, is in a phase of rapid advances." He believes that air ions are biologically active: That is, they influence a variety of life forms, from airborne bacteria and fungi to humans.

The British office workers were thought to be responding to negatively charged air molecules—particles naturally abundant around bodies of water, particularly waterfalls. These ions are removed by air-conditioning and forced-air heating systems. Consequently, the office environment may not be the most conducive for mental performance. But the ill effects of ion-depleted air predate the modern windowless office. In several parts of the world, seasonal winds cause a widespread mood shift that affects thousands of people each year, and ions seem to be responsible. In Israel, it's the *sharav*, in Germany and Switzerland, the *foehn*, and in America's Northwestern states, the chinook. These winds have been blamed for depression and irritability, as well as for physical ailments, and their unusual ion levels may be responsible. Dr. Krueger notes that when the *sharav* buffets Jerusalem, some 30 percent of the population feel the effect.

It is supposed that these tiny, invisible ions may change our moods and improve our performance by influencing levels of the neurotransmitter serotonin. In fact, the malady caused by regional dry winds has been labeled "serotonin irritation syndrome."

Fresh Air, Fresh Thoughts

In experiments with rats at the University of California, Berkeley, Marian Diamond, Ph.D., and others have found a connection between levels of negative ions in the air and of serotonin in the brain. The higher the ion level, the lower the serotonin level. Much as sunlight entering the eyes is thought to suppress the hormone melatonin, so fresh and unpolluted air may cause a lift in spirits and mental performance. Dr. Diamond also reported that rats exposed to negative ions developed larger brains. And several studies have shown that the animals learn better, and have less anxiety. These rats were simply running mazes in a laboratory, not learning Italian, of course. Nevertheless, the experimental results support the experiences of people who simply feel and work better when bathed in negative ions.

In experiments with humans, elevated negative ion levels relieved depression and sleepiness, and helped subjects maintain a high level of performance throughout the day, whereas people typically experience a falloff of competence past late afternoon. Positive ions, on the other hand, aggravate that decline.

In conclusion, the traditional office seems to be a less-than-ideal setting for mental work. Not only is the lighting apt to offer too little of the spectrum, as pointed out in the previous section, but offices can be quite noisy, and even the air may carry particles that adversely affect neurotransmitter levels. Your office mates themselves may be dragging down the quality of the indoor environment. Dr. Krueger says that several people can cause the total ion count in a room to drop "at a fairly rapid rate," contributing to headaches and feelings of lassitude and fatigue.

The above studies notwithstanding, the final word on the importance of air ions isn't yet in. Sceptics include Jonathan Charry, Ph.D., whose research on ions over the past few years has made him less of a believer. He has yet to find a mechanism through which ions might affect behavior and concedes only

---

Levels of Negative and Positive Ions

The various microenvironments we pass through vary greatly both in the ratio of ions and in the total number of ions; both factors have significant biological (biochemical) effects. Note that healthful, invigorating "clean mountain air" and the atmosphere just before and after a storm are

continued

highly charged with ions, relative to the oppressive, "dead" air in a windowless room or closed vehicle.

Air	Ions		Total	Ratio
	Posi-tive	Nega-tive		
Clean mountain	2,500	2,000	4,500	1.25:1
Rural	1,800	1,500	3,300	1.2:1
Urban	600	500	1,100	1.2:1
Prestorm	3,000	800	3,800	3.75:1
Poststorm	800	2,500	3,300	0.32:1
Light industrial plant	400	250	650	1.6:1
Office or apartment	200	150	350	1.33:1
Windowless room or office	80	20	100	4:1
Closed moving vehicle	80	20	10	4:1

Source: Reprinted with permission from Charles Wallach, *The Ion Controversy* (International Bio-Environmental Foundation, 1984).

that ion generators help to clear indoor air of pollutants. Dr. Norman Rosenthal, who is investigating the effects of light on behavior and mood, calls the evidence on air ions "soft." But Dr. Krueger points out that other extremely subtle environmental factors—magnetic fields, to name one—also trigger biological responses in ways that aren't fully understood.

Until more is learned, you could experiment with your own immediate environment. Perhaps the easiest way to introduce an optimal balance of ions into your workspace is to open the window. According to figures published by the International Bio-Environmental Foundation, the ion balance is at its worst in offices and closed moving vehicles. (It's also noticeably oppressive in the minutes before a storm breaks.) The great outdoors generally provides a good balance of negative and positive ions, especially "clean mountain air"; the best ratios occur following a storm.

Generate Your Own Ions

Another alternative is to invest in a small, quiet machine that produces negative ions for indoor environments. You can buy ion generators for under £50, although some models run considerably more. They're sold as air purifiers, and may be equipped with an activated-carbon filter. All work in pretty much the same way: Electrical current runs through a metal element to spawn billions of negative ions. Check the sending capacity (or SK) of a unit before buying it; this is the measure of its power. To reduce the ion level in an office or room, shop for a unit rated in the neighborhood of 35 to 45 SK. A smaller, 10 to 20 SK unit will treat the atmosphere in a small car. Have the dealer test to make sure that the unit isn't malfunctioning and putting out unhealthful ozone gas. You yourself can quickly test to see if an ion generator is working by turning it on and holding your hand an inch or so from the ion emitter. You should feel what seems like a cooling air current—even though the generator does not chill the air. Another test is to light a cigarette and hold it next to the machine to see if the smoke disappears. If the model flunks either test, don't buy it.

Time Warps

In the course of countless sunrises and sunsets, animal species have adapted to the rhythm of the cosmos. Humans are no exception, but we are the only animals to subject the mind and body to 21- or 27-hour days. Jet travel throws off the age-old internal clock: Fly east, and your day is compressed; fly west, and your day will be extended. The result may be jet lag, a tired and disoriented feeling that is now known to be more than the consequence of too little sleep and too many on-board cocktails (although these factors may aggravate jet lag).

When travel throws off our circadian rhythms, our overall mental performance drops. Memory, judgment, and motivation all suffer, often at a time when we can least afford the mental sluggishness—when transacting business, struggling with a new language, or making change in an unfamiliar currency. Worse off are commercial pilots assigned to longitudinal routes; relative to pilots who fly north and south and cross few, if any, time zones, they may seem prematurely aged.

Most of us naturally run on a day that's a little longer than the 24 hours marked off by the sun, and so the day-stretching effect of east-to-west travel generally is less troublesome. And your internal clock won't be thrown off by travel north or south.

Not everyone is brought down when their days are shortened or lengthened. An estimated 15 percent of the population aren't affected, including Eskimos, whose exposure to extraordinarily long days or nights seems to have granted them immunity from jet lag. And for those of us who normally have trouble getting to sleep or waking up because our internal clocks run a little fast or slow, air travel may actually feel *good*.

You can do several things to avoid or overcome jet lag. Once on board, lay off alcohol and tobacco—they further deprive you of oxygen in a pressurized cabin that may have thin air—and get some sleep. Once on the ground, heed the maxim, "In the morning, when going east, do the least; in the morning, when going west, you're at your best." According to researchers at Oregon Health Sciences Center in Portland, you can help bring your cycles into proper alignment by taking in plenty of outdoor light early in the morning if you've just traveled west, or late in the day if you've traveled east. Allow one day of recovery time for each time zone passed, says Lee Weston in her interesting book, *Body Rhythm* (Harcourt Brace Jovanovich, 1979). But she notes that a marathon jet journey through 12 time zones upsets the cycle of the kidneys so that they may need 25 days to get back into the circadian swing of things.

Fortunately, there are preventive measures you can try *before* you take off.

Successfully Weathering Jet Lag and Swing Shifts

When your internal clock is at odds with the clock on the wall, you're apt to be brought down mentally and physically. This is what happens when we fly across time zones and when we trade day for night and back again on shift work. Symptoms include sluggishness, irritability, nervousness, and insomnia.

You can encourage your mind and body to adopt the new

time imposed upon them with an "anti-jet lag diet," developed by Charles F. Ehret, Ph.D., of the Argonne National Laboratory in Illinois. In studying the daily biological rhythms of animals, Dr. Ehret identified several daily cues that influence the body's clock. He found that the clock can be most readily set to a new schedule when the mealtime cue is made less important through eating very lightly—about 700 to 800 calories a meal. The laboratory explains that "fast days help deplete the liver's store of carbohydrates and prepare the body's clock for resetting." So-called fasting days are alternated with "feast days" for a period prior to the flight or shift change. Here's how the diet works:

1. Three days before your departure day, *feast* on a high-protein breakfast and lunch (of fish, meat, cheese, eggs, and protein-rich cereals); and for supper, hit the complex carbohydrates (meatless pasta, crepes and pancakes, potatoes, desserts) to stimulate sleep. Drink caffeinated beverages only between 3 and 5 P.M.
2. Two days before the flight, *fast* on light soups, modest salads, fruit, and juices; avoid calories and carbohydrates. Observe the same caffeine rule.
3. The day before the flight is another *feast* day. Again, drink no coffee or tea or cola except between 3 and 5 P.M.
4. The day of your departure is a *fast* day, but if you are traveling from east to west, you can fast just a half-day. If you drink coffee, tea, or cola, do so in the morning on a westward trip, and between 6 and 11 P.M. when traveling east. If possible, sleep until breakfast time at destination. The first breakfast, lunch, and supper at your destination (or in your new shift schedule) should be a *feast* at the appropriate time for your new schedule. Turn on the lights, and stay active.

Hundreds of people have found that the diet allowed them to escape many or all of the discomforts that time changes can cause. (If you are on a diet for medical reasons, clear this jet-lag diet with your doctor before trying it.)

Your Internal Clock versus Society's Clock

Our internal clocks wake us each morning (unless an alarm clock intervenes). They regulate the flow of hormones through the body to prepare us for a day of thought and action. Finally, at the end of the day, they calm us in preparation for a good night's rest.

Each of us has a unique schedule, a daily pattern that is hard to alter. Some of us are day people, at our best when the sun is above; others are confirmed night people, and do our best work when the sun is elsewhere. Some of us are quick starters, while others have to drag themselves from bed to the coffee pot. Weston relates the story of a gifted, but night-loving, engineer whose habit of falling asleep on the job caused him to be fired four times in a single year. A physician suggested he find a position in which he could work at night and sleep by day, and the man went on to be happily employed by a high-tech company that allowed him to work unusual hours.

His case is unusual—most dislocations are not so severe. Nevertheless, those of us who are even slightly out of sync with a 9-to-5 workday might be operating at less than full productivity; so, within the limits of your employer's (and spouse's) patience, you might experiment with advancing or setting back your day to see what schedule feels best. Watch out for caffeine—it can throw off circadian rhythms. So can exposing yourself to bright illumination at night. And even the slight dislocation caused by British Summer Time can impair our abilities. Each spring, when we set our clocks ahead and get up an hour earlier, the number of traffic accidents over the next week goes up 10 percent.

Adjustment comes much harder to those who work at swing shifts, changing their working hours on a rotating schedule. While some people are able to adjust to their irregular hours, 27 percent of employees on swing shifts suffer impaired decision-making ability, according to the authors of *Health and Behavior: Frontiers for Research in the Biobehavioral Sciences* (National Academy Press, 1982). These workers tend to be less productive and more prone to accidents, and they are apt to sleep poorly and take more days off for illness. Worst off are workers whose schedule changes every week—an unsettling influence that may leave them dependent on sleeping pills or alcohol to fall asleep at unaccustomed times. Less-frequent shift changes, of three weeks, have been found to be easier on workers, permitting them to adapt to a new sleep pattern. Better yet is flex-time, a system that allows employees to pick their own eight-hour shifts, with better job performance as a benefit.

Mind Allergies

Sherry Rogers, M.D., a physician practicing in Syracuse, New York, encountered an engineer in his twenties who became "so mentally confused and depressed in the morning after brushing his teeth that he could hardly find his way out of the bathroom." In a sense, the man was fortunate that his symptoms were severe enough to drive him to seek professional help in finding the cause—chlorine fumes rising from the tap.

Sleuthing the substances responsible for mind allergies is the work of practitioners in Dr. Rogers's specialty, clinical ecology. It's a job made difficult by several factors. First, the culprits are among a vast number of chemicals in the environment. As many as 2,000 new ones are created each year, according to the journal *Immunology and Allergy Practice* (September/October, 1982). An arsenal of some 2,700 chemical additives is used to enhance the flavor, color, texture, and shelf life of processed food, writes Cecil Collins Williams, M.D., in the journal *Annals of Allergy* (August, 1983). Some of these additives are listed on the label, but others are known only to the processor. And an allergen doesn't have to have a long, technical name to cause trouble. Many foods can make people listless and foggy-headed, even *wholesome* foods like berries and cheeses. Literally nothing can be ruled out in looking for the responsible allergen.

We tend to be more familiar with the *physical* symptoms of the so-called traditional allergies triggered by dust, pollen, animals, and natural fibers. These substances have been causing running eyes and noses for centuries. But a second group of substances—chemicals, foods, and food additives—are hardest on the mind. According to clinical ecologist Alan Lieberman, M.D., of North Charleston, South Carolina, "Of all the organ systems in the body, the brain is the most common target of an adverse reaction to the environment."

Allergy Facts

- An estimated *one person in three* is allergic to something in the environment.
- *Anything* is capable of triggering an allergic reaction.
- Reactions may be suppressed by *increasing* exposure to the allergen, with the curious result that a person becomes addicted to it. That's why the foods you can tolerate the least may be the ones you eat the most.
- Allergies can affect the *mind* just as readily as they cause rashes and runny noses.

How do you know if you are troubled by a brain allergy? A checklist of the symptoms includes about every kind of mental dysfunction you could name: mental fatigue, tension, dizziness, confusion, lack of motivation, memory loss, and poor concentration. Not all mental problems can be blamed on allergens, of course. But if you suspect you may be susceptible to a brain allergy, read over these key indications described by Doris Rapp, M.D., a Buffalo, New York, pediatrician and allergist.

Are family members allergy prone? Hypersensitivity tends to be genetic.

Does your face betray these telltale signs? Eyes may have bags or dark circles (called "allergic shiners"), ear lobes may look red, and red patches may appear on the cheeks. Kids also may wiggle their legs rapidly; their faces tend to be pale; and they may repeatedly clear their throats, make clucking throat sounds, or sniffle.

Does your behavior provide other clues? "Many people with brain allergies will strike their friends as having a Dr. Jekyll and Mr. Hyde personality," says Dr. Rapp. "They may be kind and pleasant one moment and suddenly turn irritable, hostile, aggressive, angry." A curious change may take place with handwriting: Adults under the effect of an allergen tend to write smaller, while children's writing becomes large and sloppy, and may even turn backwards or upside down.

And how do you feel inside? "You may find that your performance level will vacillate from day to day," says Dr. Rapp, "depending on what you are exposed to and what you eat. Some people find that if they eat the wrong food, they can't bowl or play golf. Or someone will be cleaning house with a particular chemical and get fuzzy enough to forget to put dinner on. Others put petrol in their cars and then find that they can't think or that their coordination is off."

Of course you aren't a victim of a brain allergy simply on the basis of one or two of these symptoms. The next step is to begin tracking down the substances that may be responsible. Once you identify a culprit, you then may be able either to eliminate it from your environment, or to take steps to adapt comfortably to it.

Are You Allergic to Your Home?

You may be allergic to your home. Remember that the allergens are of two kinds, natural and synthetic. The natural ones include dust, fibers from bed coverings, mattresses, rags, and upholstered furniture. You can minimize their influence by scrupulously dusting and vacuuming, and this can be facilitated by getting rid of dust-catching knickknacks. To keep the project manageable, start with one room, cleaning it and removing whatever substances you have found to be troublesome. Other troublemakers besides dust and furnishings include pets, tobacco smoke, and gas or oil heat.

The synthetic group of allergens, those that are man-made, may affect you by "outgassing"—that is, by putting substances into the air where they are inhaled by the occupants. Often your nose can be your guide in avoiding synthetic allergens. A general rule to follow when shopping, according to Alan S. Levin, M.D., of the University of California, San Francisco, School of Medicine, is to "smell the product. The stronger the odor, the less should be your inclination to buy it." Among the worst offenders are cosmetics, soaps, deodorants, and colognes.

Less obvious but also worthy of suspicion are curtains, bedding, carpets, shower curtains, or clothing made from synthetic fibers. Chlorine is liberated into the air by chlorinated tap water and bleach. Formaldehyde escapes from plywood and insulation. Synthetic allergens are a growing problem; our homes contain more man-made things than they did a couple of decades back, and they are also better sealed and insulated in the interest of energy conservation. A tighter house retains not only its heat but also the gases of the myriad substances inside.

Allergens in the workplace may be harder to control, unless you happen to own the company. Dr. Levin singles out the photocopy machine and the video display terminal as special sources to consider if your job seems to bring out the worst in you. The first may broadcast inks and solvents; the second has been blamed for stripping negative ions from the air and spewing out ultraviolet and radio waves and X-rays. Poor ventilation systems may aggravate the problem. The ion problem can be relieved by working with a detached keyboard in a well-ventilated place, for short periods divided by breaks. You can install a grounded mesh screen, as well. As for the copier, ventilation again is important. Machines that put off fumes should be vented. If you have to use an unvented machine, you can resort to gloves and a filter mask, or prevail upon a nonallergic friend to stand in for you. Carbonless copy paper has been blamed for causing shortness of breath, headaches, and fatigue. To prevent trouble from the chemicals on the paper, use good ventilation, store paper away from work areas, and wash your hands after using the paper. Standard carbon paper is an alternative that is less apt to cause reactions.

If you need to seek professional help in diagnosing a problem or treating one that's already established, go through your family doctor to find either a conventional allergist or a clinical ecologist, who will be more inclined to investigate synthetic allergens as well as the better-known natural irritants.

Food Allergies

Some of us are allergic to the very fuel we run on—foods and beverages. Wheat, cow's milk, sugar, eggs, corn, yeast, caffeine, and alcohol are among the most frequently reported. Another likely candidate is any food or beverage you find yourself consuming a lot of; this may be a case of a "masked allergy," the symptoms of which may go unnoticed as long as your body continues to get a regular dose. If this sounds to you like an addiction, you're right. Says Dr. Rapp, people may react like heroin addicts. "If they get their fix of, say, chocolate, they feel better for a little while. But if they don't repeat the fix, they get a headache or feel fatigued or find they can't think."

To figure out if your mental malaise can be traced to something in your stomach, you can experimentally restrict your diet to foods least likely to cause trouble, such as vegetables, fruit, fish, and chicken. Allergists have called this the Stone Age Diet because it leaves out foods that entered the human diet relatively late in history, such as cereal grains, dairy products, and additives—which happen to be the worst offenders, according to Dr. Lieberman. This straightforward regimen should allow your symptoms to subside. (If they don't within a week or so, then the chances are your problem isn't caused by food.) Gradually introduce other foods one at a time, and watch for symptoms. Keep a meal-by-meal record of what you ate and how you are reacting to it. Stay away from items most likely to be allergenic, such as processed foods, those treated with additives, and canned or plastic-wrapped foods. Some doctors suggest this diet should also exclude those foods you tend to eat every day, because you may have developed an addiction to them. Says Dr. Rogers, "Unfortunately, the foods you love the most and eat the most frequently are usually the ones that are making you sick. "Tough break," she continues, "but when you see how great you feel by eliminating those foods, you'll know it's worth the sacrifice." So, during your dietary experiment, try to substitute new foods for your familiar standards. This is an informal version of what has been called a "rotary diet," and it may break the power of allergens while allowing you to still enjoy them— but only once every so often. To help ensure that you don't return to the same foods over and over, try a variety of items from within a food family, such as yams as well as potatoes, or duck and goose as well as chicken. You should rotate seasonings, cooking oils, and sweeteners; if you use honey frequently, you can even switch on and off from clover to orange blossom to wildflower and so on. In fact, Dr. Levin says that people may want to permanently shift to a diet that draws on a wide variety of foods to minimize the chance of developing a sensitivity to a particular food by eating it often.

Look Out for Lead

"Since 1945, when cars started pouring the lead out, the entire mental functioning of the United States has gone down quite a few IQ points. That's the enormous price we've paid for using leaded gasoline," says Robert W. Thatcher, Ph.D., of the Applied Neuroscience Institute at the University of Maryland, Eastern Shore. And Stephen Davis, M.D., warns of lead: "Man as a species is foolishly disseminating a poison throughout his environment which inhibits the 'survival potential' of his species."

Lead may rank as the greatest environmental threat to human intelligence. Fortunately, there is a lot you can do to sidestep this toxin. In recent years, the growing body of lead research has propelled governments into action. In the U.S., levels both in the air and in the blood have been going down since 1974, the year the EPA instituted unleaded petrol (unleaded petrol is now and will be available in a growing number of countries all over the world). The average lead levels in the U.S. dropped some 37 percent between 1976 and 1980, according to an analysis of data from the second National Health and Nutrition Examination Survey.

When the EPA considered relaxing and even dropping its lead regulations in 1972, the American Academy of Pediatricians, representing 23,000 physicians, protested the EPA's move and recommended that restrictions be further strengthened. In 1985, the EPA did just that, moving up the date for banning lead from petrol altogether from 1995 to 1988.

The main source of lead in our society remains automobile

exhaust. If you own an older car, maintain the exhaust system so that fumes don't enter the passenger compartment. If you garden near a busy roadway, you may be *eating* the lead from auto emissions: Half the airborne lead travels at least 200 feet from the roadway. A study of London gardens found that one-third of the vegetables tested contained more lead than allowed by British food regulations. Other uses of lead are being curtailed as well. The metal was once a common ingredient of paint—an inspection of dwellings in Milwaukee from 1972 to 1974 found that more than 60 percent presented a lead paint hazard. Since that time, lead has been disallowed as a major ingredient in household paints. But beware of paint applied before 1978, white and yellow shades especially.

These changes in the way lead is used will ensure that we are exposed to less and less lead. But to stay clear of this heavy metal, your strategy should involve two parts: to ingest and inhale as little lead as possible; and to reduce the absorption of the lead you do take in.

It's impossible to avoid lead altogether. This toxic metal has been broadcast over the globe, throughout the oceans and even to the polar ice caps. It accumulates in our own bodies, as well. Each of us is a concentrated reservoir of lead, containing from 100 to 1,000 times the level found in the body of preindustrial man. Fortunately, you can do much to lower your exposure.

Although lead is no longer used in paints, lead-based flakes of paint will be with us for years. They may be pried off walls and doorways and eaten by children. And paint flakes can fall to the ground and find their way into the soil. That's why children should wash their hands after playing in dirt that may have been contaminated by lead pigments. When the surface soil below a bridge in Boston was found to contain high levels of lead from flaking paint, nearly half of the children tested in the area proved to have high enough blood levels of lead to concern the Centers for Disease Control in Atlanta.

Dietary sources of lead may include shellfish, liver, kidney, and bonemeal. America's FDA has given thought to proposing a label on bonemeal that warns of lead's particular danger to infants, young children, and pregnant and lactating women. These people should take an alternate source of calcium and magnesium. Levels of lead range widely among bonemeal samples, and averaged 4.4 parts per million (ppm) in FDA tests. To put that figure in perspective, 10 grams of bonemeal at a slightly higher level of 5 ppm would deliver 50 micrograms of lead, or roughly half the maximum daily intake of lead from all sources for infants and young children. If you take a calcium supplement, the best choices are probably calcium gluconate and calcium carbonate.

Your drinking water may be contributing its burden, too, especially if the water is acidic (or low pH). Acidity encourages lead to leach out from soldered joints. A water softener helps by raising the pH, but this treatment may add unacceptable amounts of sodium. In any event, drink and cook only with water from the cold tap. Allow the water to run first thing in the morning to flush the water standing in the pipes overnight; this water is apt to contain elevated amounts of lead and copper.

You may want to have your water tested. Consult your local water authority to see whether they will test it. Drinking water can be considered significantly contaminated if it contains more than 0.02 milligrams of lead per liter, even though that is well below the current limit in America of 0.05 milligrams.

How to Get the Lead Out

There are a number of ways to encourage the lead that you do absorb to visit only briefly. Left on its own, this metal tends not to budge from the body. Some 90 percent of it is apt to lodge in the bones, where it may linger for years.

British organic chemist Derek Bryce-Smith mentions several factors that come into play here. Alcohol is thought to interfere with the liver's ability to excrete lead, and people with symptoms of lead toxicity would be wise to go on the wagon. Pectin discourages lead absorption; it is found in such fruits as apples, bananas, and the white portion of orange rind. Fatty foods, on the other hand, may increase the body's uptake of lead.

Good nutrition can be important in minimizing the effects of the toxin. And the corollary is also true: lead toxicity and its effects are aggravated by insufficient nutrients in the diet.

According to *Foods and Nutrition Encyclopedia*, children and pregnant women are the most susceptible to lead poisoning, in part because they are more apt to have deficiencies of calcium and iron. "We've found that getting enough iron and calcium is a good way to reduce lead damage" says Kathryn R. Mahaffey, Ph.D., a research chemist who studied the metal with the FDA.

A calcium-deficient diet may cause the body to draw that mineral from the bones, thereby freeing lead stored in the bones to do damage elsewhere in the body. Older people are especially at risk, because lead is liberated as the bones demineralize with aging; the resulting low-level poisoning may be passed off as the mental deterioration of old age.

Dr. Mahaffey has conducted a number of experiments that show calcium's benefits. In one, she found that rats eating a low-calcium diet had blood lead concentrations four times higher than rats eating a normal calcium diet, although both groups were exposed to equal amounts of lead.

In another experiment, Dr. Mahaffey found that rats who drank water contaminated with 12 ppm of lead and were on a low-calcium diet had tissue lead levels similar to those of rats receiving water with *200 ppm* of lead but a normal calcium intake (*Nutrition Reviews*, October, 1981). An interesting side-light: Dr. Mahaffey stresses that although the nutrients are important, eating patterns seem to be just as crucial. "An adult usually absorbs 5 to 15 percent of the lead that's commonly found in food, whereas after fasting as much as 80 percent of the lead may be absorbed. In other words, don't skip meals."

Doctors have known for some time that if iron intake is low enough to cause anemia, more lead will be absorbed. But what if iron intake is just moderately reduced—less than the ideal intake but not low enough to cause anemia? Can a minor degree of iron deficiency increase lead absorption, too? To find out, researchers fed rats either a diet just slightly deficient in iron or one that was adequately supplemented. After seven days all the rats were dosed with lead. The rats on the low-iron diet retained 30 percent more lead than the iron-supplemented group (*Proceedings of the Nutrition Society*, January, 1982).

Other researchers believe that zinc can influence susceptibility to lead poisoning. Penn State nutritionist Gary J. Fosmire,

Ph.D., has found that animals with only a marginal zinc deficiency have dramatically higher concentrations of lead in their bodies. It's possible that a zinc deficiency changes the permeability of the intestines so that they let more lead in. Dr. Fosmire notes, "Provision of an adequate level of zinc in the diet would seem to lessen the danger of [human] lead exposure."

Vitamin D discourages lead from building up in the body. And thiamine has been found to be a promising nutrient in treating lead contamination, according to Gerald Bratton, D.V.M., Ph.D., of Texas A & M University. In animal studies, he says, it "prevented the deposition of lead in all tissues examined, especially the kidney, liver, and brain."

4

The Brain Drugs:
Caffeine, Nicotine,
and Alcohol

In the futuristic novel *Brave New World*, people banish their unhappiness by swallowing so-called soma pills. The book's author, Aldous Huxley, took a personal interest in psychoactive drugs. He was one of the first to experiment with LSD. Could this drug truly expand the mind? Could it throw open the doors of perception and let pure reality pour right in?

Today, medical researchers continue the quest for brain drugs that might rid the world of anxiety, depression, and senility. Although promising candidates come up occasionally in medical journals and in the press, none has yet to surpass the popularity of the three reigning brain drugs: caffeine, nicotine, and alcohol.

Although taste and aroma figure in our enjoyment of coffee and colas, cigarettes, and alcoholic beverages, their appeal goes beyond the senses. Each is able to influence the tiny electrical and chemical transactions that take place behind our foreheads. For some people in certain situations, these everyday drugs may be able to coax better work from the brain.

Chapter 2 discussed foods that also influence the mind. But

drugs can be more powerful. They may come on fast and strong. In a number of complex ways, caffeine, nicotine, and alcohol are quick to reward their use and punish their discontinuance— which is to say that they're habit-forming, even addictive. Withdrawal can be painful. And heavy long-term use of alcohol and cigarettes has been linked both with impairment of the mind and with disease.

Governments as well as individuals have trouble reconciling the pleasurable side of these three substances with their potential dangers. In America, alcohol was banned by a short-lived Constitutional amendment in the 1920s, and in the 1980s many states raised the legal age limits for drinking. Caffeine first came under a critical public eye in the 1920s, and renewed concern over its ill effects is behind the current proliferation of decaffeinated brands of coffee, tea and soft drinks; but the government has yet to regulate its use. In America in the 1960s, a highly publicized Surgeon General's report on the hazards of smoking precipitated a steady decline in the popularlity of that habit, and yet the government subsidizes the tobacco industry.

Millions of us continue to use one or another of these drugs, especially when our minds are under stress. Even for professionals involved with the science of the mind, the brain-drug habit can be tenacious. Richard J. Wurtman, M.D., of MIT, perhaps the best-known researcher in the field of brain nutrition, continues to enjoy his coffee. And the first item on the agenda of the 1983 Whole Brain Symposium was a coffee hour. This chapter should help you manage your own use of caffeine, nicotine, and alcohol. It explains just how each favors or hampers the brain's transactions, balances risk with benefit, and suggests how the addicted can get off the hook.

Caffeine: The Number-One Brain Drug

Back in the early 1900s, the American government required the Coca-Cola Company to remove the cocaine from its best-selling brew of cola nut, coca leaf, cinnamon, vanilla, nutmeg, lime juice, and lavender.

But the government overlooked another psychoactive drug, one that remains in cola beverages to this day—caffeine.

Does it sound a little hysterical to call caffeine a drug? Then stop to consider for a moment how we use caffeinated drinks for their effects on mind and body. Legend has it that coffee was first consumed by a priest in an Arabian convent—not to savor its taste and aroma, but so that he could stay up and pray all night. Today, the coffee pot is an indispensable fixture in most offices. A cup or two of coffee seems to give the burst of energy sought by office workers each morning, as well as by long-distance drivers through the night. And in your own life, you may find yourself drinking a caffeinated beverage to gain a slight edge on a mental task, such as holding a meeting, writing a letter, or filling out a tax form.

To caffeine are attributed powers, too. Athletes routinely use caffeine to stretch their endurance. Some people find they can chase away a minor headache with a cup of coffee. And for asthmatics, a caffeine drink may make breathing come easier.

These people aren't imagining caffeine's powers. Its effects are actually many and varied. Within minutes of being ingested, caffeine stimulates the adrenal glands to release hormones which energize the central nervous system, and the brain's cortex—your intellectual center—in particular. Small wonder, then, that Coca-Cola was first marketed as an "intellectual beverage" and "brain tonic." Worldwide, some 100,000 tons of caffeine are consumed annually in the form of coffee alone, making it the world's most popular mind drug.

Just 100 milligrams of caffeine, about the amount in a strong cup of coffee, has been found to substantially increase wakefulness and clarity of mind, as measured by test scores. Thoughts may come more easily for a while; decision time may be shortened; and some people find they can better focus their attention on a task (*Journal of Applied Nutrition*, vol. 33, no. 1). Finally, drinkers of coffee, tea, and cola can temporarily stave off fatigue.

What Goes Up Must Come Down

So much for caffeine's benefits. The tally of the drug's less positive side effects is longer. Many regular caffeine users find that they pay for a short-term lift with a case of the long-term blahs.

Heavy caffeine use is the most common cause of cases of fatigue brought to physicians, according to New York physician Martin Feldman, M.D. In the *Journal of Orthomolecular Psychiatry* (vol. 13, no. 1), he writes that some two-thirds of new patients who come to him with complaints of fatigue drink three or more cups of coffee or tea each day.

Not everyone who enjoys caffeinated beverages becomes a slave to them, but caffeine is addictive. What's more, withdrawal can be a painful experience. Perhaps one person in ten is addicted to caffeine, reports the *British Journal of Addiction* (vol. 78). Symptoms of caffeinism include irritability, insomnia, agoraphobia (fear of going outside), light-headedness, irregular heartbeat, nausea, vomiting, and diarrhea. Heavy caffeine use can also have profound effects on the emotions, mimicking anxiety neurosis, even psychosis. In studying the effects of caffeine on college students, Kirby Gilliland, Ph.D., of the University of Oklahoma, found that the coffee habit seemed to be related to what he terms "life disruptions," including anxiety and depression. Caffeine may "degrade day-to-day living," says Dr. Gilliland, to the point that some people need professional help or even hospitalization.

But you don't have to be driven to the verge of emotional collapse to qualify as a victim of caffeine. For many people, regular use may lead to a side effect that's relatively minor but naggingly persistent: a headache. Headache caused by high caffeine use "probably is one of the most overlooked syndromes in medicine today," according to John F. Greden, M.D., writing in the *New England Journal of Medicine* (June 24, 1980).

A strong cup of black coffee is the traditional tonic to brace drinkers for the drive home from a party. But this folk remedy is based on a dangerous fallacy: While coffee may work as a short-term stimulant, it cannot reverse alcohol's impairment of your psychomotor function (*Clinical Pharmacology Therapeutics*, vol. 31, no. 1). In other words, that cup of coffee you drink for the road only makes you *feel* competent to take the wheel. In tests of psychomotor response at Britain's Hull University, subjects followed vodka drinks with two cups of coffee, either regular or decaffeinated. Those drinking the coffee with caffeine made nearly twice the number of errors.

Recent evidence also debunks caffeine's popular reputation as a brain booster. In a study of 1,500 college students, moderate to high caffeine consumption was found to be linked with poor academic performance (*American Journal of Psychiatry*).

How Can You Tell If You're Hooked?

Do you suspect that regular caffeine use is to blame for your fatigue, mental fogginess, or morning precup headaches? The evidence may be simple to gather. Just try quitting for a few days and see if it hurts.

Typically, if you are dependent on caffeine you will experience a withdrawal headache approximately 18 hours after your last cup of coffee or tea. The pain is likely to become more intense for 3 to 6 hours, and may persist for a day or longer. Caffeine-withdrawal headaches are most common on weekends, incidentally, because workers at home aren't likely to have a big coffee urn to tap through the day. Similarly, at one yoga retreat in western Massachusetts, coffee drinkers commonly experience a headache after a day of the center's caffeine-free regimen.

Working with his caffeine-dependent patients, Dr. Feldman has found other clues to a damaging dependence on caffeine. An early-warning sign of caffeine abuse is a period of dizziness when a person first stands up after lying down. Normally, blood pressure rises when a person stands, as the heart pumps blood against the force of gravity to the brain. But the blood pressure of a victim of caffeine addiction may actually drop, says Dr. Feldman. The lull in blood flow to the brain is experienced as dizziness.

Other symptoms are more subjective, says Dr. Feldman. "You don't have any energy in the morning, even though you've slept the proper amount the night before. You get tired in the late afternoon, and you have to nap." Patients also may report diminished concentration.

Once caffeinism is diagnosed, Dr. Feldman guides patients through a five-step remedial program. Although he doesn't like to use the word "addiction" to describe a destructive reliance on caffeine, he acknowledges that "people who are taking more than four cups a day have a very, very hard time getting off it."

If you are a heavy caffeine user, you may find yourself a victim of other problems that are equally apt to discourage your brain's best efforts. At the department of psychology of Kentucky's Centre College, researchers observed that caffeine withdrawal can cause anxiety, which is in turn relieved by taking more caffeine, in a pattern that "may contribute to the maintenance of regular caffeine use" (*Science*, vol. 209, no. 4464).

A third vicious cycle has been described in the *New England Journal of Medicine* (July 29, 1980): Victims of caffeine headaches are driven back to their drug for temporary relief, thereby reinforcing their habit.

How to Get Off the Hook

If you decide to kick your caffeine habit, don't go cold turkey. University of Oklahoma researcher Kirby Gilliland suggests gradually tapering off over two or three days, and substituting other beverages to ease the psychological dependence on a cup of coffee at customary times of the day.

Take heart: Millions of people have given up coffee, or at least cut back, according to a study by the International Coffee Organization. Between 1962 and 1982, the per capita consumption of coffee in the U.S. fell dramatically, from 3.12 cups a day to just 1.92. This drop has been caused in part by the increasing sales of soft drinks, many of them contributing their own doses of caffeine. And thanks to decaffeinated coffee, you can have your cup and enjoy it, too. A growing number of coffee drinkers are turning to decaffeinated brands.

Perhaps the best way to stay away from caffeine is to deal with the personal problems that may drive you to drink it. "If you're nervous or stressed, you can work on that," says Dr. Feldman. He recommends that his patients learn to handle their stress through biofeedback, meditation, counseling, or simply talking with their spouses.

If you find that the caffeine in an early morning cup of coffee or tea really helps to clear out your mind's cobwebs, you can still avoid the genie in the pot by keeping yourself to a single

Decaf Delectation

For a cup of coffee that won't tamper with your mind's work but still pleases the palate and nose, try brewing a cup from decaffeinated beans. In a taste test conducted by the *New York Times* (August 1, 1984), brewed decaffeinated coffee rated better than instant. And at Rodale Press test kitchens, 8 of 12 drinkers of brewed coffee actually preferred decaffeinated samples to regular. Better still may be brewed decaffeinated espresso, a dark-roasted coffee with a characteristic bitter taste and complex aroma.

cup. You may find help in this hint from a fellow coffee-drinker: Rather than zipping through the day on many cups of insipid coffee from the office pot, take time at breakfast to brew a single, small cup of home-ground espresso. Its exceptional taste and aroma—and not just the jolt of caffeine—give you a good start on the day.

Nicotine

If you've given up smoking or are among the 60 percent of smokers who have tried to and failed, then you know how stubborn the nicotine habit can be. What hooks smokers? Recent studies suggest that they are addicted to nicotine's effects on the brain.

Nicotine is a poisonous substance that has long been used as an insecticide and rat poison. But the minute doses taken by the smoker can cause temporary improvements in mental performance, including alertness, capacity to carry out repetitive tasks, and both accuracy and speed in an information processing test. Researchers at the University of Reading in England have observed that smoking is used by workers as an aid in tasks requiring thinking and concentration. Some smokers find that cigarettes perk them up much like a cup of coffee.

Smoking works as "a coping response to the demands of daily living," says Ovide Pomerleau, Ph.D., professor of psychiatry and director of the Behavioral Medicine Program at the University of Connecticut. He points out that nicotine has the curious ability to either stimulate or soothe a smoker: "If one feels not too alert, one can take the drug; and yet if one wishes to calm down, one can take the same drug, perhaps increasing the dosage a bit, taking it a little more quickly over time." Inhaled as smoke, the dosage of nicotine can be controlled much more closely than other drugs. And Dr. Pomerleau points out that nicotine reaches the smoker's brain even faster than if it had been injected into a vein—within just six to eight seconds after inhalation, giving the smoker near-immediate reinforcement of the habit.

Dr. Pomerleau and others believe that nicotine works by stimulating the release of neurotransmitters and neurohormones. Light a cigarette or take a chaw or dip some snuff, and you are tampering with your brain's chemistry.

At low doses, nicotine stimulates the release of beta-endorphin, an opiate made by the body. Consequently, smokers feel calmer. In contrast, a high dose apparently prompts the release of noradrenaline, adrenaline, and dopamine. Smokers may experience a lift, or find themselves in the paradoxical state of being both more alert and more relaxed. Nicotine has also been credited with improvements in mental performance through an increased release of two neurotransmitters involved with memory function, acetylcholine and vasopressin.

These brain-stimulating effects don't last for long—from 15 minutes to a half-hour. Nonsmokers who light up will simply get dizzy, not smarter.

Clearly, smokers and other tobacco users face a dilemma: They have become dependent on a drug that presents a threat to life out of proportion to any temporary benefit it might cause. Dr. Pomerleau suggests smokers try to supplant their habit with regular aerobic exercise. This is a habit that, like smoking, increases the release of beta-endorphin, acetylcholine, and adrenaline. The result of a good aerobic workout is that same paradoxical state of relaxed alertness. And unlike smoking, the fitness habit won't increase your risk of cancer and heart disease.

A Thinking Person's Guide to Alcohol

Ethyl alcohol is a clear, colorless liquid created as a waste product by certain anaerobic bacteria. That doesn't suggest that alcohol is much of a treat for the senses, and when taken straight, it's not. But despite its humble origin, alcohol is a gifted chemical. Depending on how much is consumed, it can act as a food, a drug, or a poison.

For some authors and artists, alcohol seems to coax the muse out of hiding. Writer E. B. White once mentioned in a letter to a friend that a single dry martini could effectively dislodge his occasional writer's block. How is it that alcohol may help people stymied by a blank canvas or sheet of typing paper? The answer may be in this drug's special ability to simultaneously lower anxiety and increase arousal: *Physiologically*, it acts as a depressant, reducing motor function and causing a feeling of relaxation; *psychologically*, it makes people feel high (or creative or outgoing or brave) by blocking certain inhibiting mechanisms in the personality. Studies of the elderly suggest that a drink can improve morale, mood, and energy level, and thereby allow them to make the most of their remaining abilities. So without increasing our personal inventories of wit, intelligence, or creativity, alcohol may at least allow these qualities to shine through. It is said of many disciplines that peak performance can be had only by not trying too hard; perhaps this is where alcohol comes in. A small, occasional dose may keep our anxieties and eagerness from spoiling our best efforts.

Here is a tally of alcohol's physiological effects on the mind's work. At low dosages, the drug increases the excitability of neurons; it elevates levels of acetylcholine, a neurotransmitter (or brain chemical) involved with memory function. Alcohol also gives us a quick flush of energy, as does the sugar that accompanies it in mixed drinks, beer, and sweetened wines such as sherry and port.

The Three Faces of Alcohol

It might seem that if a little nip of alcohol helps, then a few more drinks would really open the floodgates of creative energy. But in fact, these effects are temporary, and more does not mean better. After an initial period of stimulation, the brain's cells become less active; acetylcholine levels drop, then stabilize; and the brief alcohol/sugar energy boost is followed by the inevitable onset of fatigue. What's worse, alcohol has a split personality, and its uglier side comes out as the dosage increases. Take a few sips of wine with a meal, and alcohol is metabolized as a food, without creating much of a stir in the brain. Have a couple of cocktails on an empty stomach, and alcohol takes on a new personality—it travels through the bloodstream as a drug, cheering and relaxing some drinkers and dropping others into depression or even violent anger. Drink still more, and alcohol becomes a poison, with symptoms ranging from the well-known hangover to temporary amnesia, unconsciousness, and death. Tolerance varies greatly from person to person. Some individuals become sick on as little as a beer or two.

As for alcohol's power as a creativity drug, its reputation is largely a myth. It is not safe to assume that a glass of Pernod, for example, will confer upon you the creative spark of the young Hemingway who sipped this yellow-green liquor as he wrote in the cafés of Paris. And it is downright dangerous to infer that heavy drinking is a key to artistic success, despite our many cultural heroes for whom alcohol abuse was a central and at times colorful part of life. (See chapter 7 for more on creativity and alcohol.)

The trick of staying on alcohol's friendly side is to drink just enough and no more. Unfortunately, to call it quits once you've reached the optimum point can take plenty of self-control. Because alcohol is both addictive and readily available, it can be a difficult drug to use wisely. Further, many of us may feel pressured to drink in certain situations: Drinking is not only socially accepted, but at parties and conventions and business luncheons its use may be expected. The challenge here is to know yourself—your tolerance, and your personal reactions to alcohol as food, drug, and poison. You should also be aware of how much food you have under your belt to buffer alcohol's entry into the bloodstream. Finally, you should know your drink, and how much alcohol it contains.

Does Alcohol Really Pickle the Brain?

Drinkers often cheerfully acknowledge that a binge costs them millions of brain cells. It's common knowledge, after all, that our brains have untold billions of cells, of which we use only a fraction.

Until recently, medical opinion might have gone along with this popular assessment. But studies now show that alcohol is a neurotoxic agent at lower doses than was previously recognized. It does in fact destroy brain cells. Although the blood-brain barrier protects the brain from many substances, alcohol seeps right through. Animal studies suggest it can then destroy the dendrites branching out from the brain's neurons. Even light to moderate drinking may impair such high-order cognitive processes as abstracting, adaptive ability, concept formation, and learning ability, according to Ernest P. Noble, M.D., of the UCLA School of Medicine. You might call that a pretty steep price to pay for the use of any drug.

Memory suffers, too, report researchers at the Oklahoma Center for Alcohol and Drug Related Studies. They found that relatively small doses of alcohol can cause somewhat pronounced and consistent impairment of memory. Perhaps you've witnessed this for yourself, when trying to remember conversations from a party the night before. Or, you may have gone beyond a couple of social drinks and experienced a blackout— temporary amnesia without losing consciousness. (Blackouts are not at all rare. One survey of middle-aged social drinkers revealed that 30 to 40 percent had experienced them.) For drinkers at any stage of life, alcohol aggravates the toll that getting older takes on memory. Apparently, drinking interferes with the brain's ability to process new information and commit it to memory. And if you think a drink or two enhances your experience of the world, you are deluded; alcohol actually slows reaction time to visual and auditory stimuli, and it dulls the

Don't Drive Drugged

We all are coming to appreciate the fact that alcohol interferes with our ability to drive. Less well known is that certain medications can also steer us in the wrong direction.

Studies suggest that over-the-counter and prescription drugs may be a factor in as many as 25 percent of all traffic fatalities. Tranquilizers appear to be the biggest culprits, increasing odds of traffic injury or death by as much as fivefold. But a wide variety of medications can have adverse effects, some to an even greater extent than legally intoxicating doses of alcohol. Driving tests done recently at the Southern California Research Institute, for example, showed that the tranquilizer diazepam (Valium):

- Impaired the ability to track (remain in one lane)
- Impaired the ability to maintain a constant speed
- Increased the distance required for stopping suddenly
- Increased the time required to recognize exit signs
- Decreased peripheral awareness (the ability of drivers to notice things not directly ahead of them)

What's more, these impairments were just as pronounced after eight days of diazepam administration, suggesting that users develop no tolerance whatsoever to the drug.

Valium is by no means alone in being a traffic hazard; all of the medications listed below have shown evidence of adversely affecting driving performance. Sedatives for inducing sleep can be particularly dangerous because some have the ability to remain active in the system long after their sleep-enhancing properties have worn off—a hazard for early-morning commuters, for sure.

What can be done about the problem of drugging and driving? Researchers currently are working overtime to identify more specifically those medications whose dan-
continued

gers are greatest, and they plan to make improvements wherever possible. In the meantime, however, the responsibility lies with you and your doctor. Ask your doctor about any potential driving complications a prescribed drug may present. And if the medication you use is an OTC (over-the-counter) product, pay close attention to how it makes you feel: Anything less than 100 percent alert should be reason to steer clear of anything with an engine.

Experts meeting at a conference sponsored by the Merrell Dow Pharmaceuticals company identified the following over-the-counter and prescription medications as having potential to impair driving performance. Remember, this list includes only a few of the drugs that are prescribed:

- Centrally acting analgesics, or painkillers (codeine)
- Anticholinergics (Robinul, Cogentin)
- Antidepressants (amitriptyline hydrochloride, Marplan, Concordin)
- Antihistamines (Optimine, Dimotane)
- Some antihypertensives (Ismelin, Eutonyl)
- Tranquilizers (Valium, Librium)
- Sedatives/hypnotics (Seconal, Nembutal)
- Antipsychotics
- Stimulants

The experts emphasized that the detrimental effects of these drugs (such as drowsiness, loss of coordination, or difficulty concentrating) may be especially pronounced in the elderly and almost always are made worse by alcohol.

senses so that drinkers find it harder to discriminate between light intensities and between sounds.

Alcohol's effects range all over the body, and may indirectly impair the mind's ability. Down in the intestines, from which some 80 percent of alcohol is normally taken into the bloodstream, the drug interferes with the transport, absorption, and utilization of nutrients. Further nutritional havoc is caused if drinking displaces important foods from a person's diet. At the same time, the underfed body produces fewer digestive enzymes, rendering the drinker less able to digest food properly upon resuming a better diet.

Alcohol may be the oldest sleeping aid in use, and some studies suggest that it really does work. Other researchers have found that too much alcohol may reduce the quality of sleep by disrupting breathing patterns. Consequently, the brain will not be at its best the morning after.

As you age, alcohol's potential for damage grows. Without drinking more, you can expect to experience greater impairment as you pass the age of 40. Compounding this damage is the harmful interaction of alcohol with medications that older people are apt to take. In *Alcohol and Old Age* (Grune and Stratton, 1980), the authors report that alcohol-drug interactions may cause symptoms that mimic senility and the confusion of old age. While certain drugs interact additively with alcohol, antihistamines among them, other drugs are supra-additive; that is, the impact of alcohol and drugs is greater than the sum of the two. These drugs include barbiturates and methaqualone. A supra-additive reaction can cause severe depression of the central nervous system, then coma, and finally death by respiratory depression.

Add to this grim evidence the fact that drinking is implicated in high blood pressure, cirrhosis of the liver, upper gastrointestinal cancer, and birth defects, and you can appreciate that alcohol does far more to the human organism than prod the brain cheaply and legally. The drinks you take to lubricate your creative machinery may instead be destroying the works. Few people would speak out against E. B. White's nostrum of a single martini. The danger is in deluding oneself that knocking down a few more will enhance one's competence. Just as this fallacy has cut short many a driver's life, it has derailed the careers of many creative people.

5

How to Build a
Better Brain

The past several years have seen a quiet revolution in the way people maintain their bodies. Millions have learned the remarkable changes they can make in their appearance, strength, and stamina through regular exercise and sane nutrition. They are challenging our idea of what a body looks like at 40, 60, or 80.

A second revolution, this one involving the mind, is waiting to happen. The requirements are the same: regular, balanced activity. So is the goal: to go on enjoying the flexibility and strength we all experience when very young.

Just like a muscle, the mind will atrophy and stiffen if it is not exercised frequently. Now there is evidence that the brain grows stronger—even physically larger—with regular use. Remarkable new studies in neuroanatomy suggest that the adult brain sprouts new connections between cells in order to meet the demands placed upon it by a stimulating environment. The bottom line is, activity can spare you from the mental fog that prevents some older people from making the most of life. The brain is *not* an organ that ceases to develop when we leave our teens.

Why is this such a well-kept secret? One reason is that *mental* improvements are much harder to monitor than the *physical* kind. For example, if you take up jogging for a couple of months, the improvements will be looking at you in the mirror. What's more, these changes can be accurately monitored with instruments we all own: the wristwatch and the bathroom scale.

Mental Muscle

The brain builder, on the other hand, doesn't have such obvious benchmarks to offer encouragement along the way to intellectual fitness. You can't look in a mirror and see boredom, or withering creativity, or a lack of confidence in learning new skills. And as for the benefits of mental exercise, a person has to learn to savor subtler rewards than a flat tummy or a new personal best time for the half-marathon.

The mental equivalent of muscle might include an ability to shed prejudices and look at life anew; a growing facility for foreign languages; the knack for tossing off witty, entertaining letters to friends; an enviable recall of names; and an insatiable curiosity that makes you wish you could live a thousand years. None of these reawakened abilities is apt to inspire the applause of friends and onlookers. Still, most of us know and admire at least a few older people whose lively, inquiring minds are an inspiration—and we delight in their company as well.

A second reason the mental-fitness revolution has been a long time coming is that we are fatalistic about mental fortune: If a person remains sharp at an advanced age, we think it's luck. We assume that once we've become fully grown physically, the brain is full-grown as well. After all, everyone's heard the bad news about the brain sloughing off a few million cells each day. And the word is out that raw intelligence peaks between the ages of 16 and 20. Finally, we face the specters of retirement, possible senility, and a role on the sidelines of life.

A third reason is a misconception that researchers shared

How Important Is
Your IQ?

The term IQ (or Intelligence Quotient) makes some people anxious. They see it as a lifelong label that translates neatly into "dumb" or "average" or "smart." But an IQ is, before all else, a score on a test. The score was originally arrived at by dividing a person's test score by the score that people of that age would be expected to get, then multiplied by 100 to get rid of the decimal point. So, if you did better than would be expected, your score would be more than 100; and if you did less well, the score would be less than 100.

Here is an example:

$$\frac{110 \text{ (your score)}}{100 \text{ (average score for your age)}} = 1.1 \times 100 = 110$$

This pat way of arriving at an Intelligence Quotient easily led to labeling people as above or below average intelligence—"an inference that is a long way from observations of the child's actual . . . behavior," writes George S. Welsh in *Creativity and Intelligence: A Personality Approach* (University of North Carolina at Chapel Hill, 1975).

with the general public until recently: that the brain grows rapidly in the first years of life, and then settles down for the long, gradual slide to old age. Today, the big news in neuroanatomy is that the nervous system will continue to grow, if you place demands upon it. Your environment shapes your mind. And although you didn't have anything to do with the smarts you *inherited*, you can shape your environment to a considerable degree.

Here is a new twist on the saying that, at age 50, you've got the face you deserve: The motto of this chapter might be that, by mid-life, you've got the nervous system you've earned.

"The brain can change at any age," says Marian Diamond, Ph.D., a neuroanatomist at the University of California, Berkeley. Her work with laboratory animals, as well as a peek at slices from Albert Einstein's brain, has shown that the brain is designed to respond to stimulation, and will expand its powers to meet new challenges. Aging can be a *positive* event, rather than a period of mental decline.

Teaching Old Rats New Tricks

In the 1960s, Berkeley researcher Mark Rosenzweig and associates discovered that the brains of laboratory rats showed physical changes when the animals' environment was "enriched" with toys such as ladders and wheels, as well as with other rats for company. Their brains were larger by 4 percent than those of a group of rats that had been raised in an environment without special toys or other rats (despite the fact that the impoverished-environment rats became plumper). Other researchers have found that stimulating environments increase the growth of connections between cells, and that the bigger brains translate into better scores on behavioral tests.

Dr. Diamond's subsequent work showed that the brains of older rats will also respond. Her research included rats that were 600 days old, an age that roughly corresponds to 60 years in humans, as well as a group that were 766 days old. Stimulation was provided by a number of objects that the rats could explore, and these props were periodically exchanged for new ones. Further, there were ten rats per cage, whereas the nonenriched rats were placed in pairs in smaller cages.

In examining the brains of the stimulated animals, Dr. Diamond found brain growth even in the oldest rats. "These results showed the cerebral cortex remained structurally plastic throughout the lifetime of the organism," she reports in *Experimental Neurology* (no. 87, 1985). The findings "are more impressive when one considers that the animals lived in nonenriched environments for the major part of their lives before being transferred to the more stimulating conditions."

That's good news for rats. But does the human brain respond in the same way? Dr. Diamond believes so, and she bases this opinion in part on her study of the brain of no less a thinker than Albert Einstein. According to an account in the *New York Times Magazine* (July 28, 1985), his brain had been sitting around all these years in a box in a freezer behind a beer cooler in Kansas. Dr. Diamond and her associates asked for pieces from a particular area of the brain that they figured was most responsible for Einstein's genius in physics. And indeed, they found evidence that the glial cells, which support and nourish nerve cells, were present in greater numbers than in similar sites of other brains.

Theirs is not the first attempt to find physical clues to mental ability in order to lend support to a link between smartness and brain structure. Back in the 1920s, Lenin's brain was cut into 34,000 slices and studied at the request of the Soviet government. One researcher claimed to find signs of development that could explain the leader's "unusual powers of intuition."

In the *New York Times Magazine* article, psychiatrist and Yale lecturer Walter Reich says Dr. Diamond's "leap from the brain of an environmentally stimulated rat to that of a human mathematical genius is scientifically perilous." But Dr. Diamond believes that enough is known about the brain's capacity for growth to extract a few practical lessons.

How to Set Off "Dendritic Fireworks"

The Berkeley researchers found that an adult rat's brain can be induced to grow by providing the animal with things to sniff and crawl on, as well as a few other rats for company. But this isn't likely the sort of environmental enrichment that would suit you. What activities are thought to be effective for humans?

There is no set of magically effective mental calisthenics that can be prescribed. It is important to plan "new beginnings," says Dr. Diamond, whether this be volunteer work, memorizing poetry, or learning a new language. You can make up your own program of mental rejuvenation, says Jeanine Herron, Ph.D., a neuropsychologist at California Neuropsychology Services in San Rafael. She, too, believes that learning a language can be particularly invigorating. The long-term process of memorization and retrieval can set off "dendritic fireworks," according to Arnold Scheible, Ph.D., professor of anatomy and psychiatry at the University of California, Los Angeles.

If learning languages is not your idea of a satisfying way to spend a lot of time, don't force yourself. Almost any activity can help, says Dr. Herron, as long as it challenges you, requires you to make decisions, to take action. When the activity becomes automatic, then it's time to find another project to which you can apply your mind.

Watching the tube doesn't qualify, in Dr. Herron's judgment. Television allows the mind to remain passive, and is not apt to cause the brain to grow. Dr. Herron comments that she personally hasn't felt the need to worry about mental stagnation; she is an active person by nature, and is stimulated by her work. But in later life, the transition from a demanding job to an unstructured day can allow areas of intelligence to lie fallow. Dr. Herron has coached her mother and other older relatives on the importance of keeping the mind challenged throughout life.

Older people aren't the only ones whose mental powers are at risk from parking their bodies in front of a television set. Declining scores of spatial intelligence among high school seniors have suggested to testing experts that something is changing in the lives of young people today. That something appears to be television, reports a researcher at the Educational Testing Service in Princeton, New Jersey. More time spent in front of the tube may mean less time spent building models, sculpting in clay, and pursuing other hobbies that involve manipulation of three-dimensional objects. An indication of this change in the leisure time activities of young people is the decline in sales of hobby supplies, according to a report in the New York Times (August 15, 1985).

In 1980, seniors got the same spatial intelligence scores that high school freshmen had 20 years before. The impact has gone beyond the matter of testing. Howard Vreeland, Ph.D., a civil engineering professor at Columbia University's School of Architecture, has observed that today's architectural students are less able to work with spatial problems than those of past years.

Another mind-building habit that has taken a beating from television is reading. Books are highly efficient packages of information and fantasy, but apparently many adults did most of their reading back in school. In 1984, the publishing industry journal *Publishers Weekly* (May 25, 1984) reported a survey of Americans' reading habits; when asked if they had read a book the day before (the Bible not included), only 20 percent of the men and 22 percent of the women surveyed answered that they had.

Reading is among the activities that seem particularly useful in keeping mental skills sharp, according to a 28-year study conducted by researchers at Pennsylvania State University. Some 3,000 subjects of all ages gave information on their jobs and off-hour experiences, and were tested for problem solving, spatial skills, language ability, and adaptability to change. Penn State's K. Warner Shaie, Ph.D., professor of human development and psychology, found that an active, intellectually stimulating life was associated with an undiminished ability in these areas. Sadly, for those whose experience was not so rich, Dr. Shaie found a "marked decline" (*Geriatrics*, February, 1985).

Particularly beneficial were those activities that draw on a person's problem-solving skills, such as puzzles, Scrabble, and interactive computer games. Even square dancing can help, because it's one of those "activities that force you to engage in a complex pattern," Dr. Shaie explains.

Use it or lose it. Not even the nose can escape this imperative! The sense of smell of professional perfume sniffers has been found to decline more slowly over the years than that of the general population. And now researchers have found that *physical* exercise confers benefits upon the mind as well as the body.

A Powerful Mind in a Fit Body

What makes runners run?

That was the question psychologist Michael L. Sachs, Ph.D., asked of 540 runners. Surprisingly, the most common motivation wasn't to shed a few pounds and improve muscle tone, but to shed stored-up anxiety, depression, and guilt. Other people turn to exercise to simply clear out the cobwebs, or specifically to renew their creativity.

These benefits aren't imaginary. The mental effects of regular exercise are profound and extensive, touching our intellect, our memory, and our emotions. If you exercise regularly, no doubt you've experienced this for yourself. And the benefits have been confirmed formally in many studies.

At Washington University in St. Louis, 32 subjects were given a battery of tests of mental function and personality traits. After they took part in a ten-week program of jogging, calisthenics, and physical recreation, they were tested again. In *Medicine and Science in Sports and Exercise* (vol. 10, 1978), the researchers noted significant improvements in intelligence, speed of performance, learning, and brain function. On top of this, they observed decreased depression and anxiety among the group.

Other studies have shown that benefits extend to memory, attention span, and motivation. Lump all these abilities together, and you have a pretty good definition of intelligence. In other words, exercise is good for the brain.

And the opposite is just as true. Physical *inactivity* seems to numb the mind. Patients confined to long periods of bedrest become mentally lethargic, for reasons that haven't been established. It is known that physical inactivity is accompanied by electrical and chemical changes in the brain—a gradual winding down of the dominant brain-wave frequency, and decreased levels of two neurotransmitters, dopamine and noradrenaline.

Exercise, for Those Who Think Young

Researchers have been impressed by the fact that these cerebral changes are also brought on by aging. Walter Bortz, M.D., finds this parallel between inactivity and aging to be "striking." Writing in the *Journal of the American Medical Association* (September 10, 1982), he recounts a personal experience that dramatized for him just how closely disuse of the body can mimic the effects of growing old. His leg was placed in a cast to allow a torn Achilles tendon to heal; when the cast came off six weeks later, it revealed a stiffened and withered leg that looked like it belonged to a person 40 years older. For Dr. Bortz, this graphic change was a visual clue to the unseen changes which must simultaneously take place in the brain. "Physical inactivity can also prematurely age the central nervous system," he concludes.

So, the enemy of mental vitality isn't growing older, really. The enemy is the passivity that tends to creep up on us as we age.

Happily, there is plenty of evidence, clinical and personal, that an exercise program can reverse this mental decline. Says George A. Sheehan, M.D., a New Jersey cardiologist well known for his writing on running, "The fight . . . is never with age; it is with boredom, with routine, with the danger of not living at all. Then life will stop, growth will cease, learning will come to an end."

The mental benefits of exercise are hard to put into words,

Don't Act Your Age!

Why do people tend to settle into a sedentary lifestyle as they age? An obvious answer is that they simply feel less like kicking up their heels as the years go by.

But that's not the only reason, according to Andrew C. Ostrow, Ph.D., associate professor of physical education at West Virginia University. He asked some 500 physical education and nursing students for their ideas on which physical activities were appropriate for healthy men and women at ages 20, 40, 65, and 80. The students responded that no activity was appropriate for those at 65 and 80, not even walking!

Small wonder that older people park themselves in a comfortable chair. The remedy is clear: Don't act your age. You can't afford to, not if you value your wits.

but in *Running and Being* (Warner Books, 1978), Dr. Sheehan is able to hint at the good things that take place upstairs when he hits the road. "There is all the while a stream of consciousness, a torrent of ideas, coursing through my brain. One idea after another goes hurtling past like so much white water."

We tend to overlook these cerebral events because the physical changes are so much more obvious. Just take off your clothes in front of a mirror, and there you are: The fitness habit cheats time by toning muscles, melting away love handles and double chins, and returning to the face the glow of childhood. Many of us have witnessed the transformation that can be worked by taking up running, swimming, or another form of aerobic exercise—either on our own bodies or those of friends.

But over a lifetime, the mind can keep its vitality long after the body has begun to stiffen and slow down.

Dancer Gwen Verdon has put this truth simply with the saying, "Dancers die twice." That is, while few dancers (or athletes) are able to stay at their peak past their thirties or forties, and "die" professionally, most of us can continue to keep our minds operating at a high level well into old age—if we keep active, physically as well as intellectually.

That's something fitness author John Jerome learned first-hand when he decided, at age 47, to take up competitive swimming. As Jerome explains in the book *Staying with It* (Viking, 1984), he began swimming those countless laps to maintain the vitality of his nervous system, and not simply to keep physically fit. "What aging takes away—the thing I didn't want to let go of—is not so much gross physical capability as it is sensitivity, the availability of acute nerve endings. My senses have given me such vivid pleasure in the past that I am not about to accept their dulling so easily."

And he discovered, as he invested hours in the pools of local YMCAs, that exercise can win back mental powers that had been lost to disuse. It's the "use it or lose it" phenomenon, also known as the training effect. Explains Jerome, "The training effect is the small, common biological fact that says that if you ask a living organism for more, the organism will, within reason, respond. . . . To age, on the other hand, is to begin asking less." In other words, aging and physical exercise are at opposite

When Age Reels
You In, Resist!

"Range of motion is the perfect metaphor [for aging], because here is how age finally gets you: It reels you in. The mechanism is so clear it's unnerving. I recently observed a not terribly active 75-year-old who spent three weeks in bed with a very sore back. Tests have demonstrated that three weeks of bed rest will decondition even the best-trained young athletes. We don't think very much in terms of deconditioning when it comes to inactive 75-year-olds, but that's exactly what it did to my friend. It was as if she were tumbled forward—in age—at an accelerated rate.

"Once she was up and about again, it was clear that she had converted a lot of lean muscle mass into fat. (She gained no weight, did increase in bulk, lost a great deal of muscular strength.) She didn't feel like doing much, and when she did, she suffered from shortness of breath, dizziness, and general fatigue, all of which discouraged her from attempting to do more. It discouraged her from doing what she needed to do to regain what she'd lost. In short, she came back slowly, and didn't come back all the way. Her *range*—from the distance she could walk to how far she could reach to the very nature of the aims and ideas she was willing to entertain—was noticeably shortened. Nature was pulling in the string. Another illness, an injury, a reduction of activity of any sort, will pull the tether shorter yet.

"Age is clever that way. It is not that it pulls so hard, but that it is so vigilant. It is very patient, having more time than you do. It monitors you. Allow any slack—anywhere—and age, like a spider, will snatch it up and bind it in place with newly rigid, inelastic connective tissue."

Source: *Staying with It* by John Jerome. Copyright © 1982, 1983, 1984 by John Jerome. Reprinted by permission of Viking Penguin, Inc.

poles, physiologically speaking: When a part of the body or mind is allowed to slow down, aging advances a step.

No matter that the precise physiological mechanisms in the body and brain aren't known. Many people, like Dr. Sheehan and Jerome, have discovered in mid-life that keeping active is a key to regaining the vitality and growth they knew in their youth.

How much exercise is enough? You don't have to be a competitive swimmer, like John Jerome, or endure the 26-mile marathons that George Sheehan delights in. In a study on the anxiety-reducing effects of exercise, the researchers remark that your routine can be more flexible than is sometimes recommended. Twice a week is enough, they report in *Physician and Sports Medicine* (vol. 11, no. 4), and apparently there's no real harm done by having back-to-back exercise days—good news for those who have to squeeze in their exercise on weekends. A second study, in reporting 14 to 27 percent lower scores on scales of anxiety, depression, and hostility for males who took up running, notes that the number of miles jogged was not so important as the simple fact that a person got out there regularly (*Sport Psychologist's Digest*, vol. 5, nos. 4, 19).

John Jerome finds that he can prepare himself for intense periods of writing by a process known as "taper," a strategy prescribed for better sports performance, and one that seems to serve the mind as well. He finds that distinctions between mind and body are largely artificial, and that even with a cerebral task like writing a book, "the better the animal you are coming into it, the better you'll perform."

Jerome explains that taper involves a schedule of progressively shorter workouts for a couple of weeks before the physical (or mental) contest. The idea is to exercise hard but not long, so that the body is toned without working it to the point of exhaustion.

Of course, you can't taper off unless you already have been putting in a fair number of hours of exercise each week— perhaps 30 to 40 miles of running, says Jerome, or the equivalent. His schedule goes like this. Two weeks before he's ready to "bust his hump," Jerome trains especially hard for three or four days. He then gradually reduces this load by perhaps 10 percent each day, leaving him inactive a couple of days before hitting his writing assignment. Although a person is doing less and less over this two-week period, each workout session should bring the body's systems close to their maximum. Do speed work, do middle-distance work, do straight aerobic work over a longer distance—but knock off soon after you reach your peak in each activity, before you draw heavily on your reserves. Jerome explains that this causes the body to "supercompensate," to build up a capacity that goes untapped.

How does John Jerome feel after a taper? "Bright, energetic, on top of things. You tend to be able to roll right out of bed." This mental boost usually is good for 10 to 15 days, he finds.

The Biochemistry of Exercise

Do you feel sunnier, more optimistic, after a swim or a brisk walk around the block? There are plenty of good biochemical reasons why this might be so. Exercise influences the ebb and flow of the body's own psychoactive chemicals, in ways that can lift anyone's mood. Psychiatrist Thaddeus Kostrubala, M.D., author of The Joy of Running (Lippincott, 1976), has called running "a form of natural psychotherapy."

In a study of college students at Brooklyn College, those who enrolled voluntarily in a swimming class over a 14-week semester reported less tension, depression, and confusion than students who did not take the class (Psychosomatic Medicine, October, 1983).

It seems that the more depressed a person is, the greater the benefits. In fact, jogging was judged at least as effective as conventional psychotherapy in a study with 29 people seeking help for depression. The subjects were divided into two groups. One received therapy, and the other simply ran with a therapist, three times a week for 45 minutes to an hour. After ten weeks, six of the eight joggers had ceased to be clinically depressed, an improvement at least as good as that in the group receiving psychotherapy. Could it have helped that the patients' jogging partners happened to be therapists? Not so, say the researchers, reporting their work in Behavioral Medicine (June 19–24, 1978). They make the point that the therapists rarely spoke of a patient's depression, keeping conversations to matters of running technique.

Researchers have yet to pinpoint the cause of elevated mood in runners and others who get aerobic exercise. Many body chemicals have been named as responsible—lactate, glucose, androgens, testosterone, growth hormone, salt, chemical transmitters—but the effects are subjective and hard to quantify. The chemicals most often mentioned as a possible cause of "runner's high" and the blues-banishing power of exercise in general are the endorphins, a group of natural opiates. For athletes, endorphin levels are highest during exercise; for those of us in less-than-perfect shape, the peak comes some 15 minutes after exercising (perhaps that's why the shower after a workout can be so very pleasurable).

In his survey of the many studies done on the antidepressant power of exercise, Charles P. Ransford of Hillsdale College in Michigan finds a strong suggestion that exercise helps by bringing the activity of neurotransmitters closer to normal. (He points out that standard treatments for depression—electroconvulsive therapy, antidepressant drugs, and deprivation of rapid-eye-movement sleep—also happen to have this effect.) Three transmitters may be involved in producing the antidepressant effect: serotonin, dopamine, and norepinephrine. The last of these raises the heartbeat and may increase cerebral blood flow and metabolism.

Small wonder that people who benefit so much from their exercise regimen can be in deep trouble when an injury or travel forces a break in their action. Psychiatrist Norman Tamarkin, M.D., of Washington, D.C., observes that when a person has to interrupt a fitness routine, the symptoms may include depression, loss of self-esteem, sleeping problems, irritability, and chronic fatigue.

A person typically experiences "addiction" within two to four months of taking up running, according to researchers Earl G. Solomon, M.D., and Ann K. Bumpus in *The Psychology of Running* (Human Kinetics, 1981). A positive result is that, once they are hooked, people find it easier to maintain their exercise schedules.

Which sorts of exercise make the biggest impression on the

mind? It should come as no surprise that the more strenuous activities—those that make demands on the cardiovascular system and have aerobic benefit—will deliver better results than, say, bowling or golf. Most research has concentrated on running, but walking, swimming, cross-country skiing, aerobic dance, jumping rope, and bicycling are other good aerobic activities.

Mending the Mind/Body Split

Curiously, the news that exercise can benefit the mind has been slow to catch on even among psychologists. It seems that we as a culture tend to overlook the fact that head and body are joined by a neck.

The mind is part of the body, of course. It goes along for the ride when we jog or swim or play tennis. But the brain long has been popularly—and scientifically—believed to be immune to the affairs of the body below.

One reason for this misconception is that the mental benefits of exercise are not as easily noticed as the physical changes. Another reason is our popular stereotypes—the beefy athlete with a puny brain, at one extreme, and the intellectual with a huge egghead that wobbles atop a puny body. These images suggest that each of us has to make a personal choice between bulking up the muscles or building up the grey matter.

An article in the *New York Times* (October 3, 1981) took this myth further still, suggesting that physical disorders may actually *encourage* our best intellectual efforts. Albert Einstein, the article relates, believed his creativity was stimulated by bouts of abdominal pain that since have been traced to his gall bladder. "It does not seem to be very favorable for the imagination if one feels too well," he wrote in a personal letter in the 1940s. Sigmund Freud also was spurred by recurrent abdominal pain: "I have long known that I can't be industrious when I am in good health; on the contrary, I need a degree of discomfort which I want to get rid of." Others who suffered illness in their peak years, reports the *Times*, were the writers Dostoevski and Proust, the painter Van Gogh, and the composer Berlioz.

We have actually gotten to the point where we *expect* our

artists to have serious problems. It's as if the price of genius is a ruined body. Critic Leslie Fiedler has said that a qualification of honored writers in this culture is that they have a "charismatic flaw." Beethoven went deaf; Schumann, ironically, crippled his right hand with exercises he thought would stretch its span; jazz saxophonist Charlie Parker was haunted by a drug dependency and died in his thirties; and so on.

This notion of sacrificing the body for the sake of peak mental performance has not always been in vogue. In the golden age of Greece, the ideal was a sound mind in a sound body. The two were inseparable, and each aided the other. Then, in the seventeenth century, along came the philosopher and mathematician Descartes, who said that while the body is like a machine, the brain is immaterial. Since that time, the medical sciences have come to treat the brain as the one organ that is independent of biology's laws.

Today, researchers are fast revising this attitude. They're busy tallying the mental benefits earned by those of us who keep active throughout our lives.

The next few pages sketch briefly the physiological changes set in motion when you get in motion, and how they affect your brain.

Blood Supply

An obvious benefit of exercise is its salubrious effect on the cardiovascular system. Just like any other organ, the brain relies on the blood to provide oxygen and nutrients. The blood also carries away carbon dioxide and other waste products of the brain's busy, round-the-clock metabolism.

When the heart and veins fail to deliver, our thinking is quick to suffer. A number of studies point to cardiovascular problems as a key cause of progressive mental impairment in later years, and researchers have used regular exercise (in some studies combined with a low-fat diet) to restore an unrestricted flow of cerebral blood. Two researchers at the National Hospital for Nervous Disease in London, J. M. Gibbs and Richard S. J. Frackowiak, have established that blood flow to the brain declines an average of about 23 percent between the ages of 33 and 61. Less blood means less oxygen and glucose are made available to the brain, so that it has less energy to burn.

A pair of studies have looked at the age-slowing effects of diet and exercise on older people with circulatory problems. Both placed subjects on a 26-day program of regular exercise and meals prepared according to the Pritikin diet, which favors complex carbohydrates over protein and fats. Specifically, the diet provided 80 percent of its calories from carbohydrates, and less than 10 percent from fat—levels quite different from standard fare, with its emphasis on meat and scarcity of fiber. (Most Americans, it has been found, derive 40 to 45 percent of their caloric intake from fat.)

In the initial study, published in *Perceptual and Motor Skills* (vol. 48, no. 2, 1979), the participants averaged 60 years of age and, although most suffered from cardiovascular disease, they were walking or jogging up to 6 or 10 miles a day by the end of the program. The results: These older people scored better on IQ tests, as well as on psychological inventories that included such adjectives as verbally fluent, clear thinking, intellectually able, efficient, and perceptive. The authors conclude that the regimen of exercise and diet not only produced beneficial changes in the circulatory system, but also increased mental acuity—all within 26 days, which the paper termed a "remarkably" short period.

In the second study, this one conducted by Robert O. Ruhling, Ph.D., of the University of Utah, and Robert E. Dustman, Ph.D., of the Salt Lake City Veterans Administration Hospital, elderly, out-of-shape subjects took part in a four-month program to test the benefits of exercise. One group regularly walked at a quick pace, one group exercised with weights, and a third did nothing out of the ordinary. As you might by now expect, the first group improved their performance on eight different tests of mental ability. The weight lifters showed little improvement, and the idle group, none.

How is it that regular aerobic workouts can deliver more blood to the brain? First, a fit person's heart is more efficient, pumping a greater amount of blood with each beat. Second, exercise raises levels of high-density lipoproteins in the blood, and these are thought to clear cholesterol from the blood vessels.

Finally, exercise may reduce blood levels of certain fats that are harmful to the arteries.

Air Supply

The brain that is short on blood is apt to be short on oxygen as well. This is the most dire consequence of a diminished blood supply above the neck. Older people are at greatest risk because their lungs, as well as their hearts, tend to become less efficient over the years. Dr. Ruhling, an exercise psychologist, has focused on the ability of exercise to deliver more oxygen to the minds of subjects in their middle and late years. "It was really exciting with these people," he recalls. "They were normal, run-of-the-mill people who volunteered because they thought they'd feel better. Some were reluctant to do anything at first, but once they got going they didn't want to stop."

What sort of improvements did Dr. Ruhling and his subjects find so valuable? "Changes jumped out that you couldn't fake," he says. "Such things as reaction time. We feel that exercise speeds up the nerve impulses between brain cells." Younger people also stand to benefit from keeping active. Dr. Ruhling describes another study in which young subjects who keep fit have brain functioning patterns like those of young subjects, while sedentary people's brains have taken on the patterns of older brains.

Oxygen makes the difference, in large part. The brain needs oxygen to oxidize glucose in the production of electrical energy—the very sparks that are our thoughts and feelings. And it is believed that certain neurotransmitters are highly dependent on oxygen for their production. While the brain makes up only 2 percent of the body's weight, its demands for oxygen are enormous—20 percent of the body's share, ranging up to 50 percent when we are fast-growing children. Shallow breaths and clogged arteries may leave the brain gasping for air, in effect. Symptoms range from confusion and a lack of mental vitality to senility.

The ability of the body to absorb oxygen is so vital to life that it serves as an overall index of physical health: A measurement known as VO_2 max describes how well a person can take oxygen from inhaled air and transport it throughout the body via the bloodstream.

VO₂ max typically peaks during adolescence, then slowly but steadily wanes over the years. If you stay at the same level of activity—or inactivity—over the years, you can expect your VO₂ max to decline at a rate of about 1 percent per year. That would be a little discouraging, if it weren't for the great capacity each of us has for improvement: It's possible to turn back the VO₂ max calendar 15 to 40 years through regular exercise, according to the estimate of Walter Bortz, M.D. This agrees with the statement of the geriatric researchers who write in the *American Psychologist* (vol. 36, no. 4) that exercise programs can "reverse or arrest" the degeneration of aging in geriatric patients. (Even for older people who experience some cardiovascular blockage, the brain tends to compensate by absorbing more of the oxygen that does reach it, so that oxygen consumption may remain nearly normal.)

According to Dr. Ruhling's co-worker, neuropsychologist Robert Dustman, Ph.D., older people are especially apt to improve because exercise spurs the type of intelligence that's most apt to slip over the years—fluid intelligence, as measured by tests of performance—while helping them to hold on to their *concrete* (or crystallized) intelligence, which is the sum of what has been learned throughout life, such as vocabulary.

But the body and mind aren't only recharged by being active. They're also refreshed and strengthened by being *passive*. No, that doesn't mean an evening glued to the TV, but the passivity of sleep.

The Importance of Quality Sleep

Sleep is important if the brain is to keep ticking at its best. That's because sleep is more than just a mental vacation. When we drift off into unconsciousness each night—a process that happens in what scientists label "stages"—our brains go through a series of psychological processes that restore both mind and body. At sleep stages 3 and 4, for example, memories may be consolidated; and in dream sleep, the brain may be working out resolutions to unconscious conflicts. When any of a number of factors intrude—alcohol or drugs, a noisy or uncomfortable bedroom, stress carried over from the day—we upset the progressive stages of normal sleep, so that the mind misses its nightly regeneration.

A lousy night's rest can make itself felt in the workplace, if mental clarity is necessary to getting the job done well. An article in the business publication *Across the Board* (May, 1984) reports that many corporate medical directors are concerned over the effects of insomnia on employees, both those behind the desk (where decision making could be expected to suffer) and on the production line (where the wages of sleeplessness could be an accident). Said the medical officer of one appliance manufacturer, insomnia in the workplace is a "safety time bomb."

Loss of sleep harms some mental functions more than others. One task—free association—was actually performed *better* by volunteers who went without sleep in a study conducted for the U.S. Army. But groggy people are apt to be less attentive. Sleep researcher Wilse Webb, Ph.D., of the University of Florida, Gainesville, explains that sleep loss leads to errors because the heavy-eyed person simply doesn't care to attend to the problems at hand—not because of an actual loss of brain power. It follows that *interesting* tasks will continue to be performed quite well, while rote and repetitive chores are apt to suffer.

The accompanying box suggests a number of ways to improve your chances for quality sleep. If you have been having trouble, try keeping a journal that monitors both how you've been sleeping and your activities through the day, such as mealtimes, naps, and physical exercise. Jot down the time you retire and rise, how many hours of sleep you actually logged, and notes on the quality of that sleep. In time, you may find some hints as to how daytime events are influencing your sleep.

One good-sleep tip deserves a bit of amplification—maintaining a regular bedtime. If you doubt for a minute how vital this can be, consider these words from Charles A. Czeisler of Stanford University's Sleep Disorders Research Center: "People just don't realize how important regularity in their

---

A Schedule for Sounder Sleep

Here is some condensed wisdom on getting the most out of your night's rest.

During the Day

- Some people thrive on naps, using them to pay back for the hours of sleep lost to late-night work or play. But for others, an afternoon snooze may sabotage nighttime sleep.
- Regular exercise can set you up for a good night's sleep, and it may even reduce the amount of sleep you need, according to Allan Ryan, M.D., editor-in-chief of the *Physician and Sports Medicine*.
- Take some time out during the day to release emotional stress, whether through a mental discipline (meditation, practicing the piano, or just light reading) or through a physical outlet (jogging, tennis, yoga, or a walk around the block).

In the Evening

- Lay off the caffeine, and switch to decaffeinated coffee, soda, or tea.
- If you can do without cigarettes for only part of the day, make it the evening, before retiring. Nicotine is a powerful heart stimulant.
- A bit of alcohol may seem calming, but a few drinks

---

sleeping habit is," he says. "Hamsters and blowflies whose schedule is shifted by six hours every week in experiments have a 25 percent shorter lifespan." And if you've ever worked on a swing shift, you probably know just how the hamsters and blowflies felt!

Babies and adults alike can fall asleep more readily when provided with the familiar cues of the same bedtime and the same sleeping place. When a changing work schedule or travel across time zones makes these conditions impossible, sleep is won't make you sleep more soundly. On the contrary, alcohol upsets the rhythmic sleep patterns vital to a good night's rest. What's more, alcohol may give you wake-up calls in the middle of the night, via a full bladder.

- Vigorous exercise isn't appropriate just before bed, because it leaves the body's systems in a charged-up state for several hours.
- Starchy or sweet foods enable the brain to produce more of a natural sedative, serotonin. Snack on fruit, potatoes, corn, grain-based foods, or cereal.

In the Bedroom

- Once you've established a bedtime routine, your sleep may suffer if you disrupt it. So be aware of the importance of such seemingly insignificant habits as brushing your hair or reading a few pages before turning out the lights.
- Try making your bed a place for sleep and sex only—and not a substitute for the home office or living room couch.
- Good sex is a great sleep aid, and is more fun than a glass of warm milk or a talk show's forced conversation.
- You should avoid loud TV and fast music before retiring.

apt to suffer. One reason is that sleep patterns are tied to the cyclic ups and downs of body temperature. We sleep best when our temperature is at its 24-hour low, according to Czeisler and his associates. In their research, they placed subjects in a timeless environment—a windowless apartment without clocks or televisions or radios—and allowed them to seek their own sleep patterns. Meals were served at any time the subjects pleased, such as breakfast at 11 P.M., by attendants who were to betray no telltale signs of sleepiness. So life went, for up to six months. In time, subjects generally chose to go to bed when their body temperatures happened to be at their low point in the daily cycle (normal body temperatures may drop to as low as 97 degrees).

Sleep and wakeful mental activity seem to flourish at different temperature extremes. While we sleep best when we're cool, most of us think best when we're warm—typically, in mid- to late afternoon (see the following section, "Mind Rhythms").

This still leaves unanswered the question of how much sleep is best. The definitive answer isn't to be had, because of the considerable range in needs from person to person.

Forget the old saw about sawing logs for exactly 8 hours each night. You may need more, and you may need less. A variation of 3 hours, plus or minus, still qualifies as "normal," according to Dr. Webb. Most of us need somewhere between 6 and 9 hours, but a few individuals get by on as few as 2 without apparent loss (Thomas A. Edison is said to have been a 4-hour man). Our sleep requirement does not remain constant throughout life. Newborns sleep some 18 hours a day, while older people may need just 6 hours.

An interesting sidelight is that people apparently can adapt permanently to less sleep. That's what sleep researchers discovered when subjects who regularly got 7½ to 8 hours each night were told to sleep a half-hour less every three weeks. Most got down to about 5 hours before quitting the experiment. When the researchers checked on their subjects a year or so later, they found that the experiment had imparted a lasting effect: Rather than resume their original length of sleep, the subjects now were sleeping up to 2½ hours less each night.

Mind Rhythms

One day you open the morning mail and find an insurance policy that you really should read. But with its fine print and legal gobbledy-gook, the document simply refuses to make sense. You automatically put off reading it for a second try later in the day. Around 4 P.M., you pick it up once again, and this time your mind is able to untangle the confusing jargon with relative ease.

Sound familiar? Each of us has a pet time of day at which to tackle mental tasks, whether it's writing a difficult letter or practicing finger-tangling scales on the piano. A project that seems all but impossible at 8 A.M. may be a snap in mid-afternoon.

What's going on here? The heavens offer an answer—not in the mystical science of astrology, but in the regular appearances of that neighborly star, the sun.

There's nothing mystical about it. Many of the body's systems are regulated by an internal clock that is attuned to the daily pattern of darkness and daylight. These include heart rate, blood pressure, respiration rate, and body temperature. Animals generally are oriented to either day or night, depending on their niche in the planet's ecology. We humans tend to be at our best by day—all but a few incurable night owls among us, that is.

Not all daylight hours are equally friendly to mental work. That's because as the body's various systems gear up and downshift each day, our capabilities change too. Once you identify these personal peaks and valleys, you should be able to perform better, according to British researchers Keith Oatley and B. C. Goodwin in *Biological Rhythms and Human Performance* (Academic Press, 1971), both "in efficiency of work and in enjoyment of leisure."

It's important to know when you're hot and when you're not, says Carl E. Englund, Ph.D., of the environmental physiology department at the Naval Health Research Center in San Diego, California: "The percent differences found over the day are sufficiently great to account for the difference between an A, B, or C grade on most tests."

That's because body heat, more than other body signs, closely corresponds to your general state of mental alertness—the warmer you are, the sharper your mind, in most categories. Researchers aren't yet sure if you're sharp because you're warm (perhaps a warm temperature speeds up the brain's chemical activity) or if the two changes just happen to simultaneously respond to an internal clock of some kind. Nevertheless, you can monitor your oral temperature over a few days for an idea of when you are hitting your intellectual stride.

Dr. Englund says all it takes is an oral basal thermometer,

one that is calibrated from 94° to 100°F by tenths of a degree. It gives you the accuracy you need to chart your temperature fluctuations.

"Measure every hour during your waking day, over four or five days if possible, and you'll see a nice frequency distribution," says Englund, "a nice pattern." Don't influence the readings by having a cold or warm drink within 30 minutes of a measurement. And try to take measurements in the same conditions; that is, if you've been taking measurements lying down, continue to do so.

The personal daily peaks and troughs that you see emerging probably correspond within two or three hours of your *mental performance* pattern—they're "about as individual as a fingerprint," Dr. Englund has found. And your body tries to maintain its pattern. Miss sleep, and you force your body to shift grudgingly into a new rhythm, with mind-befuddling results similar to jet lag.

Generally, temperatures are highest in the late afternoon and lowest before dawn. Rises and falls are quite rapid, with a relative plateau between 10 A.M. and 9 P.M. Personal temperature peaks, however, range from noon to late in the evening. Those who have just flown across several time zones will be thrown off their daily schedules, and the resulting disorientation is known popularly as jet lag. (For help in overcoming jet lag problems, see page 72.)

An interesting sidelight is that personality seems to have something to do with the time at which most systems are fully in gear. Introverted people—those who score relatively high on the "unsociability" scale of a personality inventory—hit their peak levels of arousal early in the day, while extroverts are slower to warm up but remain at higher levels throughout the rest of the day.

An exception to the close link between temperature and performance is the so-called post-prandial (or after-lunch) dip in performance that hits many people in the early afternoon. Each day around the same time, they find their eyelids getting heavy. In chapter 2, this "siesta response" is traced to the effect of a carbohydrate-heavy lunch on a transmitter in the brain that induces a relaxed feeling. But in *Biological Rhythms and*

Human Performance, W. P. Colquhoun points out the curious fact that people don't seem to become dopey after breakfast or supper; in fact, a good breakfast is widely thought to *increase* mental vigor. It has been suggested that the midday drop in alertness is a vestigial response to a biological need that humans no longer have. The dip could also be a cyclical brain-wave phenomenon, of the sort observed in sleeping people.

Among the characteristics found to fluctuate daily are pulse rate, adding speed, short-term memory, counting, and word association. With the possible exception of memory, all reach a peak in the afternoon. Researchers have even noted a change in humming (the preferred pitch changes through the day) and in sensitivity to dental pain.

Predictably, night shift performance tends to be off the daytime level. Studies reveal a greater number of errors and slower response times as body temperatures decline at night. One study showed that night-shift switchboard operators took longer to respond to calls as the night wore on. And in a Swedish gas works, the accident record over more than 20 years showed that mistakes increased steadily through the night, with 3 A.M. being the most goof-prone hour of the graveyard shift.

Still, you may be able to think of certain mental activities that seem to go best in the morning. Dr. Englund explains that although some tasks in fact are performed more readily in the morning, the likelihood of errors is greater than in the afternoon, when efficiency is generally highest. So, if you're after speed at the expense of accuracy, then you may be at your best in the morning; if you want to minimize mistakes, on the other hand, as in certain tests, then you would be wise to put off the project until the afternoon. He concludes that we can compensate somewhat for our off-periods of the day, but that each of us can also learn to identify our peak times and then take full advantage of them.

Your Thoughts Can Make You Sick

An important attempt to bridge the mind/body split is the study known as behavioral medicine. This discipline brings together internal medicine and psychiatry, and its central tenet is that your thoughts can make you sick. In this highly stressed society, we all can think of case histories from our own lives or those of family and friends.

This is the flip-side of the under-exercised body providing an unfavorable environment for the brain. Here, the troubled mind can wreak havoc in the organs and systems below the neck.

These ailments are labeled psychosomatic, but this doesn't mean that the symptoms are imagined, as in hypochondria. Far from it. Although until recently only a few diseases were recognized as being caused or aggravated by the mind (asthma, ulcers, and high blood pressure, to name the best known), many others are now acknowledged. The list includes rheumatoid arthritis, colitis, constipation (or its opposite), flatulence and indigestion, menstrual irregularities, herpes simplex, acne and rashes, tension headaches, and poor eyesight. Eventually, unrelieved stress may predispose a person to hardening of the arteries, heart attack, and stroke—which together are responsible for a large number of deaths each year. Cancer, too, is thought to be hastened by long-term emotional stress.

There are several channels by which the mind keeps in constant two-way communication with the provinces below (a more complete account is given in chapter 1). Obvious paths are the central nervous system, made up of the brain and spinal cord; and the peripheral nervous system, the network that links the brain to organs and systems throughout the body.

The mind is also chemically tied in with the body. The *endocrine glands* release chemical messengers that travel through the blood to all parts of the body, including the brain, where they function as neurotransmitters. And the *endorphins* are a group of natural opiates released by the brain; in the body, they slow breathing and lower blood pressure; in the brain, they exert a calming influence by blocking the transmission of pain signals.

Other mind/body messengers are adrenaline, known as the "emergency hormone," and noradrenaline. While these stress hormones increase the force and frequency of heartbeats, they also can increase mental alertness—as is appropriate in a stressful situation. But a constant state of arousal can be counter-productive.

Keep Stress from Sabotaging Your Mind

Sometimes we find we work better when we're under the gun. The stimulus of a big deadline sends adrenaline flowing through the veins, and this can temporarily spur us on. Adrenaline speeds the heartbeat and increases the flow of blood to the brain.

Although adrenaline can be valuable in preparing us for occasional bursts of great output, it can undo our powers of concentration and memory; it may even cause muscle tremors that make it difficult to speak in a steady tone or write legibly. This you already know, if you've ever stumbled over your tongue when speaking in public, or felt your mind go blank when pressed for an important name or number. In other words, it's possible to try too hard. Stage fright and writer's block are two of the better-known symptoms.

Stress closes down the lens of our attention. While that is appropriate in an emergency—say when looking for a fire exit in a blazing theater—this so-called "tunnel vision" blinds us to much of what is going on around us. We are apt to miss important things that were said at a meeting, or we may fail to notice a stop sign coming up.

An urgent need to succeed can sap our attention from the job at hand, whether it's interviewing for a good job or just playing a board game. The compulsion to wrestle with life in this way is a symptom of "Type A" behavior. Here are a few key symptoms that describe a Type A personality:

- Driven to pursue unrealistic goals
- Engaged in a losing battle against time
- Unable to delegate authority because fellow workers are seen as inadequate
- Has a hostile attitude toward others, justified by the conviction that they have it in for you

Stress also causes us to tighten up physically. Muscles become anesthetized and lifeless. This can be disastrous in sports, as when tense, uncooperative limbs send the tennis ball sailing over the foul line. The mental equivalent of tight, twitchy muscles is a self-conscious mind that harshly critiques every thought before we get a chance to speak it or write it down.

To judge by the number of stress-management books on the market, many of us feel the need to improve our performance by calming down, rather than by getting psyched up. How can you keep your response to stress from interfering with your work? The suggestion, "Relax, don't take life so seriously," is easily prescribed but hard to follow. Fortunately, you have the choice of a wide variety of stress-management techniques that can redirect your energies in a positive way. These include meditation, biofeedback training, exercises in muscle relaxation, yoga, and massage.

Meditation

Meditation means many different things, ranging from taking a moment to collect our thoughts to highly structured forms of Eastern meditation. The mind/body benefits claimed to be results of meditation include reduced stress, faster reaction time, and greater perceptual ability. One study, printed in the *International Journal of Neuroscience* (vol. 16, 1982), suggests that meditation may even slow the aging process. Subjects practicing the Transcendental Meditation (or TM) method were compared with nonmeditators on three biological indicators of aging's effects: measurements of hearing, near vision, and blood pressure. For each subject, a biological age was calculated and then contrasted with his or her actual, chronological age.

When the statistics had been worked out, it appeared that "long-term" TM subjects—those meditators who had been at it the longest—had a biological age that was an average of 12 years younger than their chronological age; those who had been meditating a relatively short time scored 5 years younger on average; and controls, who did not meditate, averaged 2.2 years younger.

Just how does meditation accomplish this? Other studies

have pointed to changes in the central nervous system. Specifically, meditation may improve a person's signal-to-noise ratio; that is, the mind works more efficiently when it has less ongoing mental chatter, or "noise."

Westerners may find themselves uncomfortable when facing an exotic meditation system. It may take you a bit of searching to find a method that fits into both your daily schedule and your beliefs. Transcendental Meditation borrows from Eastern meditation, while seeking to explain and validate its benefits through Western medical studies. The TM approach is not inexpensive, but it does offer a widely available, standardized technique. The TM student is assigned a mantra—a phrase in the Sanskrit language—that is to be repeated silently as a means of gently directing the thoughts. In follow-up sessions, TM teachers check to see how the new student's practice is coming along.

The initial popularity of TM was followed by the appearance of stripped-down techniques for people who want the benefits of Eastern meditation without the trappings of incense and gurus. Cardiologist Herbert Benson, M.D., and psychologist Patricia Carrington, Ph.D., have developed systems from which they have pared away anything that could be construed as mystical or devout. And they have simplified directions to the point that a person can learn the methods from a book or tape, without the presence of a teacher. Whether or not this is enough guidance for a novice meditator is a matter of the person's individual makeup. Some people may prefer the structure of more traditional methods.

Dr. Benson's brand, called the relaxation response, involves a mantra (the syllable "one") that intentionally lacks an exotic flavor. Twice a day, the meditator sits comfortably in a quiet place and repeats the mantra silently. That's it. The method is simple—perhaps too simple, admits Dr. Benson. "Many do not believe something can be worthwhile that is both free and safe," he says.

Dr. Benson is characteristically straightforward in explaining how the relaxation response works. He doesn't call up the traditional notions of Nirvana or mystical ecstasy, but describes meditation as an application of behavioral medicine: that is, as a technique that can help a person manage the mind/body phenomenon known as the flight-or-fight response.

As you may already know, this response is the body's automatic way of preparing for danger, through a release of adrenaline and noradrenaline. It is a healthy reaction, so long as the increased level of hormones translates to physical action, whether that be running away from the threat or doing battle with it. More often in our civilization, however, we just sit on our anger and fear, and allow the emotional storm to brew within. The storm makes itself known through all kinds of physiological thunder: elevated blood pressure, pounding heart, sweaty palms, loose bowels, tense muscles.

So, while the flight-or-fight response can save our lives, or lead us to peak periods of output, it may also get us in trouble— as it did for a relief pitcher who was about to make his first appearance in the major leagues. When the young man was called in to replace the starting pitcher, he climbed into the stadium's car for the short drive to the mound. It's a trip of only some 500 feet, but along the way his flight-or-fight response got the best of him and he vomited.

That's not a promising way to begin a major league career. And while this story is remarkable for the degree of the man's panic, he's not alone in mishandling stress on the field. One major league ball club has taught all of its players to meditate.

Dr. Benson prescribes meditation for his cardiac patients, along with drugs and psychiatric counseling. He recounts the case of a 39-year-old man who suppressed his anger to the point that his heartbeat became irregular and he collapsed and turned blue. Meditation helped this patient manage his reaction to stress, and gave him an aid that he could continue using after stopping the drugs and counseling.

Dr. Carrington's method is called clinically standardized meditation, or CSM. It too is purged of anything that might be seen as mystical. However, she provides more support and instruction than Dr. Benson, through her book *Freedom in Meditation* (Doubleday, 1977) and a cassette course with a 94-page workbook (Pace Educational Systems, Inc., P.O. Box 113, Kendall Park, NJ 08824). She offers a variety of mantras, and suggests how to pick one that will work best. If problems should arise in picking up the meditation habit, she troubleshoots the likely cause. The tapes hold your hand through each step, but the book is written clearly enough that it may be just as effective.

Biofeedback

A modern technological version of meditation is biofeedback. In fact, biofeedback can be thought of as "machine-assisted meditation," explains Ken Pelletier, Ph.D., a clinical psychologist who specializes in stress management. Using apparatus that monitors brain waves, muscle activity, or other bodily functions, a person can learn to control heart rate, blood pressure, and skin temperature, much as an Indian yogi does. When the subject manages to alter a biological state, such as muscle tightness, the machine provides the immediate "feedback" that the change has in fact taken place. This technique is used to treat such mind/body problems as high blood pressure, heart disease, gastrointestinal problems, and migraine headache.

The biofeedback approach to stress management isn't for everyone. "Why use a machine for something you can do naturally with your thought patterns?" asks Herbert Benson in his book *The Mind-Body Effect* (Berkley Publishing, 1980). The technology may actually *increase* anxiety about performance, he has found. But for some people, biofeedback apparently works because they are impressed with the high-tech hardware, rather than turned off by it. The electrodes, blinking lights, and dials inspire their faith, explains psychiatrist Richard Goldberg, M.D., of Rhode Island Hospital, writing in *Annals of Internal Medicine* (April, 1982).

Linking Mind and Body

As I write this page, my hands are cold and stiff because of the draft from a poorly sealed window above the desk. So, I will consciously warm them, using a method I recently learned with the help of biofeedback technology.

Fifteen minutes later, my hands hit 92 degrees, as monitored by a ring thermometer, and they feel as warm as they might if I were sitting on a sunny beach.

This is a neat trick, of value to those of us who naturally tend to have cold hands. And it's one of a number of bodily states that anyone can learn to control. Blood pressure, heart rate, the work of glands and the digestive tract, and the local circulation of blood—all are functions that medical textbooks traditionally have described as involuntary, but all can be brought under conscious control.

These functions are monitored by the sympathetic nervous system, the unconscious part of the brain. It's fortunate we don't *have* to constantly concern ourselves with running them. The sympathetic system minds the store for us.

But there are any number of reasons why we might want to step in and take control—reasons that send many people to learn techniques from biofeedback practitioners to solve problems that include not just cold hands, but high blood pressure, anxiety, insomnia, asthma, spastic colon, teeth grinding, and so on.

Not that you have to hook yourself up to elaborate monitors to tune into bodily signs, as I did recently. For example, an obvious clue that you're anxious is the thub-thub of a heart that's pounding mightily under the influence of adrenaline. Or a glance in a mirror can inform you that you're blushing.

But other internal states are subtler, and biofeedback devices can alert us to changes that would otherwise go unnoticed. Electronic sensors can pick up their information through inflated cuffs (to measure blood pressure), skin electrodes (to detect brain activity and the electricity discharged by muscles), or fingertip temperature sensors. They then display their messages by flashing lights, meters, or buzzers.

The theory behind biofeedback is that any bodily process that can be monitored may perhaps be one that you can learn to control. So it is with high blood pressure (hypertension). This common affliction is thought to be aggravated by emotional stress. Anger and frustration don't actually make the blood boil, but they may send blood pressure climbing. Biofeedback can help hypertensive people by revealing the intimate connection between their emotions and blood pressure levels. A pressurized cuff is wrapped around the arm and communicates to a monitor which gives a constant readout of blood pressure. Subjects are able to observe that certain emotional states raise or lower the numbers; with practice, they learn to exercise a measure of conscious control over this vital sign.

The benefits can be dramatic. The Menninger Foundation in Kansas reports excellent results among patients who have come for relief from high blood pressure. According to the Foundation's Steven Fahrion, Ph.D., some 70 percent are able to completely stop the medications they're on.

Other problems that may respond to biofeedback training include arthritic swelling, hot flashes, menstrual cramps, curvature of the spine, bowel incontinence, diabetes, insomnia, Reynaud's disease (cold extremities), and chronic muscle pain. Asthma sufferers can learn to dilate their bronchial passages. Alcoholics become able to sense the level of alcohol in the body. Blind people learn to adopt the conventional facial expressions that accompany emotions. A particularly interesting monitoring system has been used to help deaf children overcome their characteristically nasal way of talking. Nasality is determined by the position of the soft palate. A sensor wire is cemented to a molar tooth, and another is placed on the palate. The wires are connected to a monitor, which signals to the subject when he or she is successfully avoiding a nasal tone.

Another benefit of biofeedback was accidentally discovered in research on skin temperature control. When subjects with headaches consciously elevated the temperatures of their hands, they found that their headaches vanished. The temperature shift was caused by an increase in the blood directed to the hands, and apparently this diversion of blood flow reduces the cranial pressure blamed for migraine discomfort. Today, biofeedback relief is widely available. At the Hartje Stress Clinic in Jacksonville, Florida, migraine sufferers average a 75 to 90 percent reduction in pain after using this technique.

Biofeedback technology has its Eastern parallel in meditation and yoga. Through practicing these mind/body disciplines, a person learns to exercise control over body functions that are usually considered involuntary. Biofeedback researcher Elmer Green, Ph.D., studied an East Indian yogi who could voluntarily cause his heart valves to flutter so rapidly that he had no detectable pulse.

Biofeedback can help a person control the mind's own processes, as well as the body's. Aided by a monitor that picks up brain waves through electrodes on the skin, the subject can learn to shift the brain's predominant mode of thinking from one type of function to another. These states are defined by the frequency of brain waves, and are named by Greek letters (see the box "Brain Waves"). Again, this application of biofeedback technology has its parallel in Eastern meditation, which also enables a person to favor one state over another.

Many people turn to biofeedback for relief from persistent anxiety. With practice, you can learn to switch off the fight-or flight response to stressful thoughts and situations. The key is to learn to control one element of that response—skin temperature, or relaxation of a forehead muscle that's particularly resistant to control, or brain-wave frequency, or sweating at the

---

Brain Waves

Alpha: The mind is turned inward and, although still alert, is relaxed.

Beta: Attention is focused on solving a problem or some aspect of the outside world; also occurs during emotional anxiety.

Delta: Occurs during deep sleep.

Theta: Occurs when person is drowsy, and in the nearly unconscious state immediately preceding sleep. Images are apt to form spontaneously.

fingertips. Any of these can serve as a way to influence the sympathetic system.

You can sense some bodily changes without being hooked up to electronic monitors; for example, you can feel your hands getting warmer as you will the blood vessels there to relax and permit greater local blood circulation. But an electronic ther- mometer, attached to a finger, can detect fractional changes in temperature. That means you get a near-instantaneous report (or "feedback") of how your thoughts and body sensations can trigger temperature changes. You know immediately if you're doing something conducive to relaxing those blood vessels (and the sympathetic nervous system as well).

But wouldn't a person become dependent on all this expen- sive electronic hardware, and have to return repeatedly for emotional "fixes"? No. That's because the equipment isn't doing anything to you; it merely helps you to recognize when you're successful at changing a bodily state and when you're not. Once you learn which thoughts and feelings do the trick (people typically make a dozen or so office visits), you can practice this new behavior at home, independently of the hardware.

Put Yourself in a Creative Mood
with Biofeedback

Biofeedback technology can help a person shift from one style of thinking to another. One particular rhythm of brain waves, labeled by the Greek letter *theta*, is associated with the surfacing of images from the unconscious mind. Researchers at the Menninger Foundation guessed that biofeedback monitor- ing of brain waves could increase the creativity of subjects by enabling them to stay in a theta state of mind. Biofeedback pioneers Elmer and Alyce Green taught a group of 26 college students to voluntarily increase the amount of theta waves they produced, relative to the alpha waves which typically are more plentiful in a waking state. The subjects heard a high tone when they were in the alpha state, while a low tone meant that the theta was coming on strong.

Over the several weeks of the experiment, they were asked to comment on their subjective feelings in a log book and in recorded interviews. The Greens found an overall increase in theta production, and reports of increased imagery; the students also mentioned feelings of well-being, and said that they were doing better in school and getting along better with others.

What Is Biofeedback Like?

Biofeedback isn't difficult, but it does take practice. That was my recent observation after half a dozen sessions with George Fritz, Ed.D., a clinical psychologist specializing in biofeedback therapy.

For my first session, I was hooked up to a headset that monitored brain-wave activity. Grounding clips were dipped in salt water (to improve their conductivity) and placed on my earlobes. Immediately I heard a signal, a sound like the chirping of an agreeable cricket.

I was told to observe the chirps without trying to generate them. In time, I noticed what silenced the electronic cricket—daydreaming, worrying, drifting into drowsiness.

On another day, the brain-wave monitor was linked through a nest of wires to a cassette player with a tape of lovely acoustic guitar music. But there was a string attached: The player stayed on only as long as I was able to remain in an alpha wave state, sometimes described as a state of relaxed awareness.

Brain Games

There is now on the market an electronic game in which one player tries to launch a spaceship while the other tries to keep it on the ground. That sounds straightforward enough, but the novel part of this game is that the players use their *brains*, not their hands, to control the ship. Both try to wrest control of the ship. Both wear EEG monitors that pick up the dominant brain-wave frequency. The player who produces the strongest alpha waves—the frequency associated with a relaxed, alert state—gains control of the spaceship.

The instant I began to indulge in a pet worry, the machine shut off with a snap. By the end of the session, I was enjoying the music without interruption, and I left the office feeling relaxed.

Biofeedback works—if you're willing to invest the necessary time and money. Dr. Fritz says most people need 10 to 12 hour-long sessions to learn to control a particular body process. Practitioners charges will vary. And Dr. Fritz advises clients to practice their new skills at home twice daily. He finds that the people who are most successful are those who are "gently persistent," who avoid the pitfalls of impatience and frustration.

Muscle Relaxation

Another approach to avoiding stress is through muscle relaxation. Such techniques may be "homely," says psychiatrist Richard Goldberg, M.D., but a progressive tightening and relaxing of the body's muscle groups does seem to ease a troubled mind.

Just how this works is not yet known. One possible explanation is that these exercises make a person aware of the muscular tightness that is a telltale sign of emotional stress. We then can consciously try to stay loose in stressful moments. In effect, tense muscles are serving here as a biofeedback signal, and allow us to manage our stress level.

Progressive relaxation has been described widely. You assume a comfortable posture, and allow yourself enough time to clench and release each muscle or muscle group in turn, starting at the toes and working up.

Which of these paths to relaxation is best? Finding the answer to that may be as challenging as picking the best form of exercise. Different folks take to different systems.

In a study comparing the effects of three methods in reducing anxiety—Transcendental Meditation, biofeedback, and muscle relaxation—the results were surprisingly similar. The journal *Archives of General Psychiatry* reported in 1980 that, for each technique, about 40 percent of the subjects who made it through the training period reported marked improvement in managing their anxiety. Drop-out rates often are high. In the *American Journal of Psychiatry* (1980), researchers report that of students who practiced either muscle relaxation or TM, only 15 to 20 percent were still practicing regularly after 2½ years. Not everyone takes to meditation like a duck to water, explains Dr. Goldberg. Problems that may come up include the critical attitudes of others, becoming distracted, fitting daily practice sessions into a busy schedule, and finding that results come slowly.

Any system is apt to be more effective when used as part of a three-pronged approach, says Dr. Pelletier. He recommends combining the stress-management system of your choice with a program of regular exercise and sound nutrition.

If none of these systems is to your liking, here's good news. You may do just as well simply by taking a break from the daily grind. Dr. Goldberg cites a study suggesting that this may be as effective a stress reducer as any of the methods described in this section.

And a final word on anxiety: It's neither all good nor all bad. According to researcher Don M. Tucker, Ph.D., the right amount of anxiety can help energize the mind. In order to think most effectively, he says, "you may need a certain level of anxiety." So, don't look upon your anxious feelings as enemies that you necessarily have to obliterate in order to compose your thoughts.

Body Therapies

When you burn your finger on the stove, you automatically flap your wounded hand. And when tension causes your head to pound, you rub your temples or press hard into the muscles at the back of your neck.

These are simple, perhaps instinctive, examples of body therapy. Early in life, we learn that we can relieve the aches of body and mind through direct manipulation. The term most often applied to this sort of therapy is massage, and professionals have been practicing it for thousands of years both in the West and the East.

The Greeks and Romans knew the medical benefits of massage, but the practice apparently degenerated into a service rendered only in houses of ill repute. The methods were revived by French physicians, and massage was finally brought back into respectability in the early 1800s by a Swede, Henri Peter Ling. Along the way to winning acceptance, massage took on the French terms still used today, including *effleurage*, or long strokes, and the percussive tapping and therapeutic punches known as *tapotement*.

While Western body therapies have concentrated on giving the body a tune-up, the Eastern view is that the kneading and pushing of skilled hands can somehow restore the mind and spirit as well. This distinction is important to sorting your way through the dozens of body therapies available today. The Western approach is *structure-based*, explain D. Baloti Lawrence and Lewis Harrison in their useful guide, *Massageworks* (Perigee Books, 1983); the goal is simply to work out the body's kinks and aches.

Eastern forms may appear similar, in that they also use an arsenal of pummelings and proddings, but the goal is more ambitious: to restore the body's energy flow, in what Lawrence and Harrison term an *energy-based* approach to massage. In other words, the therapist's hands are also addressing the recipient's mind and spirit, not just muscle and sinew and bone. Maintenance of this energy flow is said to be crucial to physical and mental vitality.

Westerners tend to regard the Eastern approach with caution. We aren't immediately at ease with a force that can't be seen or measured. We don't even have a popular name for this force, and borrow either the Japanese *ki* or the yogic *prana* to describe it.

Here are descriptions of a few of the many therapies widely practiced today.

Although Western *massage* is more concerned with structure than energy flow, people do turn to it for relief from mental stress. In New York City, for example, some executives have a massage as an after-work pick-me-up, rather than downing a couple of drinks before the homeward train ride. Marilyn Frender, a massage therapist and editor of *Massage Journal*, says that the busiest time at her mid-Manhattan practice is from 4:30 to 6:30 P.M. each day.

Massage therapy is used geriatrically as well, notes Frender, and can be a useful part of an older person's daily agenda. In addition to relieving stress, massage is thought to improve sluggish circulation, Frender says.

Shiatsu is a form of massage brought to this country from Japan. It works on the same principle as acupuncture—but without sticking little needles into the skin. Instead, shiatsu therapists use their fingers to undo the energy blocks and imbalances that are said to form along the body's energy pathways. In theory, these problem areas form as a result of life's troubles. Among the above-the-neck benefits attributed to shiatsu are a reduction of stress and a feeling of serenity. The renewed flow of energy is said to relieve headache and fatigue.

Proponents of *reflexology* say that this form of manipulation can help erase the background noise from a tense mind, even though the pressure is applied only to the feet or hands. Reflexologists point out that they aren't performing massage (indeed, many are not licensed to do so); they simply are applying pressure to produce changes elsewhere in the body.

"We don't really know how it works," admits Gale King of the International Institute of Reflexology in Florida. But this "zone therapy," as it has been called, is said to restore both circulation and an undefined flow of energy through the body. An advantage of reflexology is that you can perform it on yourself a lot more easily than a back massage; if you can't talk a friend into kneading your feet, you should be able to reach them yourself.

King recalls that one writer came to him for treatments in hopes that they would enhance her creativity. He's not sure that she got what she came for, but he suggests that the mind is in fact a beneficiary of the technique. Reflexology is fairly straightforward, as techniques go, and two-day courses are offered to people who would like to practice it on themselves.

The benefits attributed to *Rolfing* are so remarkable that Rolfers (as the practitioners are known) take care to understate the benefits of the ten-stage "realignment" process. Richard Stenstadvold, director of the Rolf Institute in America, recalls that the woman behind the technique, the late biochemist Ida Rolf, Ph.D., was conservative when talking about her work: "I

don't want to come across as a crazy old woman," she is supposed
to have said.

So it is that she stuck to a straightforward definition of
Rolfing: using deep massage to realign a body that has become
"badly organized" through life's stresses and strains. "There is
no psychology, there is only physiology," was one of her tenets.
But privately she acknowledged that her technique went far
beyond body therapy: It was an approach for integrating the
body with mind and spirit.

Rolfers continue to speak modestly. "We can't say Rolfing
will make you smarter," says Stenstadvold, and indeed, most
people who are Rolfed are surprised to discover that the effects
encompass the mind. "We let others extol the benefits," he
explains.

The ten-part therapy may be painful at times. And although
benefits are long lasting, a person may want to come back for a
refresher if their Rolfian alignment is knocked askew by emotional or physical trauma at some later time.

Is anyone so untainted and so at ease that Rolfing is
unnecessary? Stenstadvold likes to think that, somewhere in the
world, there must be. But he says that only newborn babies seem
to have the natural pliability that is our birthright.

These are just a few of a broad range of body therapies.
None can be recommended as a specific prescription for better
memory, greater creativity, or deeper intelligence; that's
because the good effects suffuse both body and mind, and the
mental benefits are hard to tally separately. Of course, *anything*
that restores the body stands to give the mind a lift as well,
whether it be a 1,000-year-old massage technique or simply a
particularly satisfying sneeze.

The Power of Positive Thinking, Revisited

Self-help books of the past extolled the value of positive
thinking. Typically, they portrayed ambitious young people
pulling themselves up by their emotional bootstraps, to become
captains of industry and esteemed leaders.

Today, a widely used variation of positive thinking is

guided imagery, also known as visualization. By forming compelling, positive images in the mind, a person overcomes the blocks that have plagued every generation—anxiety and self-doubt.

Visualization can be put to work in any number of ways. Memory specialists employ vivid, often absurd mental images to help people remember bland names and numbers. Psychologists counsel clients to imagine themselves coping swimmingly in situations that have sunk them in the past. And physicians recognize positive imagery as a way to influence the body. Summon up certain images, and you can affect blood flow, tension in the muscles, pulse rate, and skin temperature. Learning to control these bodily states is made easier with biofeedback devices (see page 129). They monitor your physical condition electronically, giving immediate readouts so that you soon learn which images are associated with muscle tension, elevated temperature in the hands, and so on.

The objective of an imagery session may be simply to relax, to reduce muscle tension, or to perform better on the job. Imagery is also applied in a highly focused way in the hopes of acquiring cars, jobs, specific salaries, and even love partners. You can learn the technique from stress management consultants, yoga teachers, and clinical psychologists, and books on imagery and relaxation, which describe a variety of step-by-step approaches.

Not everyone will find it easy to come up with convincing mental images. It's possible to try too hard; distractions may prove frustrating; and a big dose of scepticism can keep the mental screen blank. For any of these reasons, a person may find that firsthand training works better than lessons from a book. Another alternative is a tape that takes you through each step, while allowing you to practice when and where you choose.

In their book *Directing the Movies of Your Mind* (Harper & Row, 1978), Adelaide Bry and Marjorie Bair stress that if a visualization is to bear fruit, three ground rules must be met:

- You really have to *want* the goal.
- You have to feel you *deserve* the goal.

• You have to *believe* beforehand that the session is going to work.

Picture This

"Your imagination, your capacity to daydream or fantasize, to relive the past or probe the future through pictures in your mind's eye"—these are among the "greatest resources you have as a human being," says Jerome L. Singer, Ph.D., professor of psychology at Yale University.

When you're feeling stressed, your imagination can carry you to a peaceful place through *guided imagery*. Get comfortable, close your eyes, and allow your mind to assemble a relaxing scene from the past: a forest pond you once discovered on a hike, the guest bedroom at your grandparents' house, even a reclining seat on an airplane, if that's where your mind is at its ease. Bring in sounds: birds, wind in the trees. Try to summon up smells, too, and perhaps the physical sensation of being in that special setting.

Reside there for several minutes, or as long as you can maintain the image without expending much effort. When you decide to come out of your session, do so gradually, opening your eyes and then slowly acclimatizing yourself to the world outside your imagination.

A more focused imagery session can help you with specific goals. *Imagery rehearsal* was first utilized by Richard Shinn, Ph.D., a Colorado State University psychology professor, for athletes at the school. Again, you allow yourself to relax, and then mentally rehearse a performance, as vividly as possible and with a successful outcome, of course.

People who are troubled by some aspect of daily life—such as speaking in public, talking on the phone, or writing a paper—can also make use of rehearsing a successful scene in their imaginations. A first step may be to begin by casting in the starring role a person you know to be at ease in this situation. Then, after a few trial runs, the understudy—you—can stand in. (For other tips on working with images, see the section "Visit Your Unconscious Mind" in chapter 7).

The Mind in Sports

In baseball, a .220 hitter finds himself batting at a .500 clip for one magical summer month. And a tennis player with a timid serve is suddenly able to consistently slam aces past her opponent, with a force and accuracy that astound them both. Players are apt to pass off such hot streaks as good luck, just as *bad* breaks are blamed on the weather or tendonitis or a string of unfriendly umpires. But students of sport are intrigued by the possibility of figuring out how streaks happen, with the hope that they can be made to visit more often and stay longer.

The search for an answer has taken both Western and Eastern approaches—biofeedback and laboratory experiences, on the one hand, and the Asian disciplines of yoga and Zen on the other. In the 1960s, eastern European countries and the Soviet Union began exploring *both* paths of mental training for their athletes. The results were so impressive—in the 1976 Olympics the Soviets placed first in the number of gold medals won and East Germany placed second—that other countries assumed that the illicit use of drugs was responsible. But since that time, some of these unusual techniques have come to light—methods of mental training that were initially developed in the 1950s for Soviet cosmonauts. This program is light-years away from traditional training, with its focus on the body and perhaps a pep talk for the brain just before game time. The Soviets were investigating the yogic ability to control brain-wave patterns, body temperatures, heart rate, and other bodily functions that most of us would call involuntary.

In the U.S., meanwhile, a tennis teacher named W. Timothy Gallwey arrived at a mind-control method he initially called "yoga tennis." Gallwey, a Harvard-trained educator, had noticed that players hit their peak only when they trusted themselves to do the right thing—when they were able to simply "let it happen," to relax the conscious effort to direct the ball over the net. This state has been described as "effortless effort," or in the words of Zen author D. T. Suzuki, "self-forgetfulness."

Gallwey went on to publish his observations in the best-seller, *The Inner Game of Tennis* (Random House, 1974). In it, he says that the best athletes "know that their peak performance

The Inner Game of Thinking

Timothy Gallwey, the man who taught the inner, thinking approach to tennis back in the early 1970s, now coaches business people. He uses sports as a model in teaching them how to think.

In the *Inner Game of Tennis* Gallwey told tennis players they would have a better chance of directing the ball successfully over the net if they got rid of certain counterproductive mental habits—namely, consciously trying to steer the ball's trajectory. He showed players that they could do much better by attending to the *sound* of the ball hitting the court, the *feel* of the racquet connecting with the ball, and the *experience* of the body as it goes through its moves. In other words, players were to reel their mind in from the court, and let it work in the body, where it belongs.

Trying not to try was Gallwey's key to the inner game, and now he is applying his method to the game of the 1980s and 1990s—business. Corporations hire him to teach managers how to pay less attention to maintaining an aura of competence, which is the managerial equivalent of mentally steering a tennis ball into the opponent's court. He helps them instead to adapt to new, challenging situations as they arise—or how to think on their feet, to put it colloquially.

never comes when they're thinking about it," and he uses the term "mindlessness" to label this state. Which isn't to say that a hot streak is an unconscious feat, or that the mind is lounging out there on the playing field. Quite the opposite. The mind is definitely on the job, but quietly so, without anxious thoughts about stardom or failure.

Athletes appreciate more than ever the psychological component of peak performance. In fact, competitors now travel to events with a sports psychologist as well as a coach. But you don't have to be a pro or full-time amateur to benefit from sports psychology. Here are some basic tips for getting your mind on your side of the game.

Mental Tips for Peak Sports Performance

No amount of mental preparation or psychological coaching can spare you the need to *learn the skills* and then practice them diligently. But once you are in good training, *visualize the successful completion of the event*. Make these little mind movies as graphic as possible, says Gallwey. Fill them in with the actual setting, and color in your feelings as the event unfolds. (In terms of brain science, this strategy may involve a shift from the left brain, with its control of language and reasoning, to the spatially aware right brain.)

Censor your negative thoughts. Again, vivid mental imagery can help. In *Releasing* (Morrow, 1984), Patricia Carrington, Ph.D., suggests that we can learn to abandon our stressful thoughts by first experiencing the physical sensation of letting go of a tennis ball or other small object. Similarly, the late martial arts expert Bruce Lee would banish a negative thought by mentally writing it on an imaginary piece of paper, then crumpling the paper into a ball and setting it on fire. Alternately, you can substitute a positive, constructive thought for the uncomfortable one.

You may have read of accounts in which athletes attribute their success to a newly discovered ability to *center the mind*. After winning her first victory on the Ladies Professional Golf Association tour, Muffin Spencer-Devlin told the press that she had won because of a book on yoga that she had been reading just the night before. The message that influenced her was B.K.S. Iyengar's admonition to focus on the present. "I stayed within the concept of one thing at a time," she told the *New York Times* (August 19, 1985), "concentrating on each swing as it must be made, not yesterday's or last week's. There were no distractions. I was very centered."

Root yourself in the immediate time and place by concentrating on the colors, textures, and sounds around you. In *A Life of One's Own* (J. P. Tarcher, 1981), British psychotherapist Marian B. Milner describes how she learned to shake off her inattentiveness when at the theater by focusing on a detail of the production, rather than by trying to will her mind to absorb the whole experience. Specifically, she transported her mind's eye to the stage and focused on the hem of the curtain. The next time you find yourself out of touch with what's going on around you, try a similar trick to anchor yourself in the present.

"Concentration means keeping the mind *now* and *here*," explains Gallwey. When you start agonizing over a past flubbed play, or allow yourself to speculate about what friends will think if you drop a fly ball with the bases loaded, then only part of your mind is on the game as it is being played. Gallwey suggests that tennis players keep their minds in the here and now by focusing on the sight of the ball (its seams, its trajectory), on the sound as it is smacked and then hits the ground, and on the feel of the ball as it meets the racquet.

Once you find yourself in a streak, resist the temptation to analyze it to death. Gallwey suggests in *The Inner Game of Tennis* that if you are playing an opponent who is enjoying a streak and simply can't be beaten, casually ask just what it is about his or her technique that is clicking. Chances are, Gallwey says, that you'll make the player so self-conscious that the streak will come to a sudden halt!

6

Keep Your
Memory Sharp

Forgetting is a part of life.

You forget 99 percent of everything that enters your head, and you can be thankful this is true. If every sense impression and thought stayed with you, your mind would soon become hopelessly cluttered. Important facts would be buried under ever-mounting piles of trivia.

In fact, this has been exactly the fate of a few extraordinary individuals who simply could not forget. Books on memory tell the unhappy story of Solomon Veniaminoff, a Russian journalist whose near-perfect memory became clogged with information. He left his newspaper job when he could no longer function well, and ended up working at what he did best: He took his memory act on the road with a traveling carnival.

For most of us, fortunately, the brain edits experiences. The memory retains the highlights of the millions of impressions made upon it—a nervous first date, a laughably low starting salary, the smell of burning protein as a dentist bears down on the drill. This isn't to say that the brain retains all the information you wish it would. The reason you're reading this chapter is that you've been frustrated by not being able to retrieve useful information. You are not alone. Memory books are perennial best-sellers. Corporations in America hire experts to coach executives in memory skills.

You'll be glad to know that memory, like any other intellectual power, can be strengthened. Chances are small that you will fade into a forgetful older person if you keep your mind challenged and treat it to good nutrition and plenty of rest. In *Stop Forgetting* (Doubleday, 1979), the late memory expert Bruno Furst made an analogy with building muscles: "If we realize that memory can be developed like a muscle, we must also accept the truth that its efficiency will diminish like a muscle if not properly used." That is, the idle memory will become flabby with disuse, just as a limb will atrophy if immobilized in a cast. According to Penn State gerontologist Nancy J. Treat, memory power may taper off as people retire from an active life and discontinue their personal strategies for remembering. "People do what they need to do for the task at hand," she has found, and these strategies can be relearned. Books on memory skills may work for some people, she says, but others will do better with personal methods that tend to be developed subconsciously, as the need arises.

The cardinal principle behind memory power is simple: Use it often or it will become rusty. This chapter will describe how the memory is thought to work, and then go on to suggest how to sharpen this all-important faculty, through sound nutrition, physical exercise, stress management, and a few simple techniques.

The Mechanics of Memory

How does the memory work? That's a good question and, after centuries of theorizing and years of medical research, a question still in need of a good answer.

Simply stated, memory is nothing more than an animal's record of the events that have been picked up by its nervous system. Even single-celled animals can store information. But in what form are the bits stored? And how do memories come out of storage, to form a sentence or guide a golf swing?

Plato proposed that impressions are made upon the brain much as a stylus marks a wax tablet. More recently, neuropsychologist Karl Lashley became convinced that memories were stored as electrical impressions, and he spent years futilely picking apart rat brains in search of proof. And currently, a holographic theory of the brain states that memories are stored in the brain as three-dimensional constructions.

But if there's no consensus on what memory *is*, experts do seem to agree on *why* memories are either selected for retention or allowed to evaporate. Apparently, a piece of information has to pass through three stages on its way to being stored over a long period.

1. Most of the ongoing flood of *sense impressions*—conversations, sensations of touch, the barely noticed smell of furniture polish, and so on—linger in the mind for only seconds and then vanish. That is, they *seem* to vanish: Some researchers believe these fleeting sensory memories may in fact be stored, to surface through dreams and hypnosis, or when touched surgically by an electric probe. Police investigators use hypnosis to enable witnesses to recall more of what they observed at the scene of an

---

"I Want Vanilla"

Perhaps you've noticed that, if you read flavors of ice cream to a young child at an ice cream store ("banana, teaberry, fudge ripple, rocky road, boysenberry ripple, vanilla"), the child often will pick the very last.

This isn't because the child is indifferent to the flavors; people of any age are more apt to retain the first few and the last few items in a list. That's because the ones in the middle are lost as the mind is busy assimilating those heard first, and the last-named items linger simply because they're the freshest and haven't been bumped by following items.

accident or crime. People occasionally turn to a hypnotist to assist them in remembering where they left a long-lost possession.

2. The second stage of memory is called *short-term memory*. What is special about thoughts that are allowed to reach this stage? They are selected for storage because you invest your attention in them. Your interest—or alarm or delight—makes the difference.

If that is so, then why are so many of us frustrated by absentmindedness—the inability to recall things we want to remember, or should remember? According to Thomas Landauer, Ph.D., a researcher at Bell Laboratories' Human Information Processing Department, "absentminded" means just that: The mind is elsewhere when you want it to focus on the matters at hand.

So it is that a name mentioned in a book—let's say it is Thomas Landauer of the previous paragraph—may linger only a few seconds. But if you were interested in learning if Dr. Landauer had any books in print on the subject of memory, then his name might lodge itself in your short-term memory. This stage is thought of as a trial period for memories. If an item is not soon used—that is, called forth and rehearsed—then it is probably destined to be forgotten, as quickly as within a half-minute or within a day or two.

Examples of memories that last only that long are the plots of television shows or what you wore the day before yesterday—items of passing interest, but not apt to be of use to you in the days, months, and years ahead. If an old high school friend happened to have a role in that show, or if the trousers you wore ripped at work, then the memory may well linger. In fact, this property of memory is behind the basic memory-boosting trick of associating a memory you want to hold on to with an out-of-the-ordinary thought. For example, if you want to remember the all-too-forgettable Italian conjunction *ma*, meaning "but," you might tuck the word into your memory with the thought that "Ma has a big butt." This slightly scurrilous image will help ensure that *ma* will stick, at least until you get to Italy and make that bland syllable a meaningful part of everyday conversation.

The point about rehearsal also has a practical application. You increase the chances of holding on to a piece of information if you recall it a few times soon after committing it to memory. That's why drills often are an important part of learning unfamiliar vocabulary and points of grammar.

3. If short-term memory is like a desktop upon which we sort out the more valuable information, then the next stage, *long-term memory*, can be thought of as a file. When people complain of being forgetful, they usually are referring to loss of long-term memory. And long-term memory is particularly vulnerable to impairment as we age.

Forgetfulness has a number of underlying causes, but all can be traced to a problem at one of the three stages of learning: 1, *registering* the item; 2, *filing* the item; or 3, *retrieving* the item.

If your mind is absent while you are supposedly memorizing the grocery list your spouse is reading to you over the phone, then you are stuck at stage 1. The material was never truly absorbed in the first place. As the popular saying puts it, the message went in one ear and right out the other.

Typical of a jam at stage 2 is the case in which a piece of information isn't filed because it has to compete with too much material. This explains why a study at Bradley University found background music to be anything but a helpful study aid. The sounds, even though pleasant, tend to crowd out the thoughts that are supposed to stick (see chapter 3 for information on music selections that will help, not hinder). The emotion of anxiety also carries with it thoughts that compete with the ones you hope to absorb.

Another reason information may not be filed is that the events that follow may displace what you've just learned; research suggests that material is retained best if the study session is followed by sleep. So, you might try hitting the books before a nap or, if you're not too groggy, before retiring at night.

When things go wrong at stage 3, you are unable to pull stored material out of your mental file. An example is the "tip of the tongue" phenomenon. Everyone has had the experience of knowing something well enough but not being able to access it—no small source of frustration when taking a test or introducing two friends. Older people in particular may find that retrieval becomes increasingly difficult. But memory experts suggest ways of pulling those elusive memories to the surface. Free associating can help: Just allow the mind to scan related thoughts, and you may find a roundabout way of making that memory available. It also helps to relax. Anxiety over forgetfulness can put even well-known facts out of reach, such as your prepared comments when speaking before a large group of people, or a friend's name when introducing him or her at a strained social event.

Retrieval problems are referred to as "blocks." We unconsciously put up *emotional blocks* to protect ourselves from unpleasant memories. These thoughts tend to be stashed way at the back of the mental file. They also may be revised over time to render them less uncomfortable, much as an oyster coats abrasive pieces of sand to form a pearl. Just after the painful birth of a child, a mother may declare, "Never again," and then as the memory of that pain subsides over time, the pleasant aspects of childbirth overbalance the negative and the decision is made to have another child.

A *mechanical block* is one in which the material was picked up incorrectly in the first place. In *Total Recall* (Rodale Press, 1984), Joan Minninger, Ph.D., explains that a fact may not be there because we either misunderstood it or were distracted as it was about to be filed. Another mechanical block may occur at the retrieval stage when the mind is preoccupied by a number of competing thoughts; if you are playing Trivial Pursuit one evening and the kids begin crying upstairs as your turn comes around, your recall probably will suffer.

Physical blocks may be the work of inadequate diet, illness, fatigue or anxiety, an injury to the head, alcohol, or drugs. These blocks can be overcome, if you can identify them and then make appropriate changes in your life. Other blocks may be permanent—blindness, deafness, the progressive effects of senility, and damage to the brain itself. A small area of the lower brain, the hippocampus, has been called the gateway to memory because it is thought to command another lower-brain region, the thalamus, to file memories. Dramatic evidence of the thalamus's function came at the expense of a U.S. Air Force recruit, known as N.A. in the medical literature. He was in his dorm room as his roommate was playing with a small fencing foil. The roommate happened to lunge just as N.A. happened to turn, and the thin blade passed up one of N.A.'s nostrils and pierced his thalamus. Now middle-aged, N.A. cannot hold a job because he has trouble forming new memories. He *can* recall memories stored before his accident, however.

Learning to Remember

As every student knows, learning by rote—just plain cramming facts into your skull—can be an unpleasant experience. And once absorbed, these bits of unrelated information tend to dribble out of the memory.

It's far better to learn material through understanding. If the new facts are related to other parts of your life, chances are better that they will be locked in your memory. Of course not everything we have to learn is of immediate and intimate interest, as when memorizing the periodic table or road directions. That's where mnemonic devices come in—systems that help us implant facts in our minds.

To judge from all the memory books, tapes, and courses on the market, a lot of people feel the need to use these systems. They train their memories for different reasons. According to Arthur Bornstein, of the Bornstein School of Memory Training, business people want to improve their memory for names and faces; students want to cram more facts between their ears; and older people want to rebuild what they see as a waning faculty. The school offers a home course with cassettes and a book (you can write to them at 11693 San Vincente Boulevard, Los Angeles, CA 90049).

Some particularly useful memory books are *Memory*, by Elizabeth Loftus, Ph.D. (Addison-Wesley, 1980); Dr. Minninger's *Total Recall*; Bruno Furst's *Stop Forgetting*; and *The Memory Book*, by Harry Lorayne and Jerry Lucas (Stein and Day, 1974). The first two authors are psychologists, and they explain how memory works and fails, as well as giving practical advice. The last two are strong on specific mnemonic systems, which you may find to be either a godsend or a waste of time. Mastery of these systems can stretch the memory to an astounding virtuosity. Basket ball-star-turned-memory-expert Lucas once memorized some 30,000 names and numbers from the Manhattan phone book. But these systems themselves take time to learn, and may seem tortuous or contrived to you. For example, one method for remembering playing cards would have you record a card hand with such mental images as a gigantic apple core taking a drink, a cake rocking a doll in its arms, a sock acting like a steam radiator, and so on—which could improve your game of bridge a notch, but might interfere with your enjoyment of the game.

The principle behind most mnemonic systems is simple: You make associations between the hard-to-remember material and an item already stored in long-term memory. For example, a person might memorize the chemical trichlorethylene by associating its abbreviation (TCE) with the initials of a friend. Another strategy is to make an association with something colorful, even off-color. The beleaguered memories of medical students get a break with the phrase "Never Lower Tillie's Pants, Mother Might Come Home" when learning the eight bones in the human wrist—navicular, lunate, triangular, pisiform, multiangular (greater), multiangular (lesser), capitate, and humate. A tamer phrase, "Every good boy does fine," has served generations of music students confronted with learning the notes of the lines on the treble clef.

Rhyme and rhythm are handy aids to memory and can produce good results. Consider a preschooler zipping through his or her ABCs—a string of 26 symbols. To put this feat in perspective, try memorizing a number with 26 digits! The poetic lilt and rhyme of "i before e, except after c" help to keep that spelling rule in our heads. Alliteration works, too: "Red right returning," goes the sailor's phrase for remembering that red markers should be on the starboard side when coming into port. (Of course, remembering that "starboard" is nautical talk for "right" is another problem.) Raciness, silliness, rhythm, rhyme— all are hooks that contribute to an effective association.

Do these methods build a stronger memory? Not really, according to a study at Carnegie-Mellon University. Researchers there observed the progressive improvement of a student in memorizing a string of random digits. Although he was eventually able to average almost 80 digits (compared to just 7 at the outset of the 20-month program), his short-term memory apparently was not stretched. Rather, he memorized short groups of just 3 to 5 digits each that he recalled by associating them with either running times for races or with ages. He then strung these groups into "supergroups" of no more than five each. This method worked for the specific task, but when the experimenters changed the subject's test to consonants of the alphabet rather than digits, his memory plummeted to only 6 or so letters. "With an appropriate mnemonic system, there is seemingly no limit to memory performance," the authors conclude, but "it is not possible to increase the capacity of short-term memory with extended practice."

What does this say about the worth of memory systems? That they can produce impressive results, in specific cases, without transforming a poor memory into a powerful one. And that mnemonic skills may not be transferable from one task to another, as the subject in the Carnegie-Mellon experiment demonstrated when he attempted to memorize letters rather than numbers. But you can develop the habit of devising your own mnemonic systems whenever they seem appropriate.

No two people find the same systems equally valuable. Perhaps association games will take you only so far, so that you will do well to switch your memory strategy to using a pocket-sized notebook for writing down names, numbers, and dates. Or you may find that simple repetition of the material to be learned will work well enough; audio cassette programs are handy at those times of day when a book would be inconvenient or impossible to use, such as when you're driving to work or weeding the garden. You can buy the tapes, or record your own.

And what if the cleverest mnemonic device still doesn't do the trick? Dr. Minninger, who brings a much needed measure of common sense to the memory book shelf, counsels in *Total Recall* that mnemonics is a game, to be played only if you enjoy it. "Otherwise, just make a list and look at it," she says.

Stress: Memory's Worst Enemy

One interesting study of the effect of stress on memory took place aboard a plane. Servicemen were asked to write down whatever they recalled of emergency procedures—but there was a twist. To introduce stress, the test-takers were told that their plane was about to ditch into the sea below.

Their recall turned out to be poorer than that of a control group of servicemen back on firm ground. The conclusion: Extreme stress is not conducive to recall. Your own experiences may have already suggested this. You don't have to be strapping on a parachute in a plane above the ocean to experience memory-numbing fear. If your knees are knocking with anxiety when taking an important test or speaking before a group of people, key facts may be hard to remember.

Memory expert Arthur Bornstein has called heavy stress the number-one enemy of a good memory, and he counsels his clients on ways to unwind. Drinking and smoking won't help; alcohol and nicotine are damaging to memory, and these traditional responses to stress will take you farther from your goal. Some people benefit most from meditation. Others relax with regular exercise or yoga sessions. And for those who are extremely anxious about doing their best, it may help to simply not try so hard.

How does anxiety interfere? Elizabeth Loftus suggests it narrows the focus of a person's attention so that the all-important cues that accompany memories are missed. As was explained earlier in the chapter, a memory tends to stick better if it is associated with an emotion, a sense impression, or a vivid experience—as when a woman's name is linked with the visual cues of her face and the setting in which you met her. A fact stripped of such associations can be hard to hold on to; that's why it is a challenge to memorize dry lists of foreign vocabulary. When anxiety keeps us from noting these helpful cues, we find it tougher both to store memories and to retrieve those already stored. Matters only get worse when our memory's failure under stress generates still more anxiety. Dr. Minninger calls this the "tension cycle," and says it must be broken to get the memory back in gear. Relax, and you will again be able to "free associate"—to allow your unconscious mind to search through your mental files for the cues associated with the memory you are after.

This having been said, you also should know that the opposite emotional state—unmotivated boredom—is no better. If you're indifferent to the point of feeling lazy, your memory again will prove uncooperative.

So, the optimal mood for remembering things is one in the middle—what has been called a state of "relaxed attentiveness." No doubt you have been visited by this emotional state, perhaps when playing a musical instrument, painting a picture, reading, or watching children play. The mood may be almost meditative, and in fact meditation techniques are said to reduce anxiety without simultaneously reducing the meditator to a dull stupor.

The challenge here, then, is to steer the middle path. One immediate step you can take is to prune your anxiety at the root. Public speakers have an arsenal of simple, fast-acting techniques. Try indulging in a slow, luxurious yawn and a stretch just before walking to the front of the room, or do a few slow head rolls, clockwise and counterclockwise, to relieve tension in your neck. Beware of entertaining fantasies of having either total success or abject failure; these all-or-nothing predictions, in which your audience is either on their feet cheering or else scowling in disgust, can prevent you from keeping a level head.

A standard technique in meditation is to breathe deeply and slowly, and this can be an inconspicuous way to relax whenever needed. Slow, measured breathing may also allow enough time for important points to come to mind when you are speaking in public. In her book *Speak and Get Results* (Summit Books, 1983), spoken communication expert Sandy Linver talked with Coca-Cola president Don Keough on this last point. "A lot of speakers [are] afraid to think while they're speaking," he says. "I think it's an enormous tribute to an audience to let them know that you are not only talking to them, you're thinking right in front of them." One tutor of management skills adds this trick: If she finds her mind going blank when facing an audience, she imagines that each person in the audience has a silly, pink pig's snout. The seriousness of the situation is defused and her memory can function again.

Another strategy for reducing stress, one that produces more long-lasting results, is to exercise. A regular program of exercise will help slow your breathing and loosen anxiety-tightened muscles. Just imagine walking to the speaker's podium with the same purposeful, relaxed stride that carries you from the tennis court after a couple of good sets. George A. Sheehan, M.D., a cardiologist well known for his books and columns on long-distance running, says he is an anxious person who runs to earn pockets of mental calm in which a "torrent of ideas" can pour forth.

Yoga is a millenniums-old method for reuniting mind and body. It can remedy the familiar disembodied feeling we get when we are highly anxious. Meditators also find that their practice allows the mind to become "centered" in the body. Meditation may actually increase the flow of blood to the brain, thereby supplying more oxygen.

At Stanford University, psychiatrist Jerome A. Yesavage, M.D., found significant improvement in memory among older people who were coached in relaxation techniques. The subjects, aged 62 to 83, were tested for recall of faces and names and outperformed a control group, presumably because their state of calm alertness allowed their memories to function more efficiently.

"Anxiety and worry actually clutter your thoughts and decrease your thinking ability," Dr. Yesavage says. "We talk about processing capacity, which is the amount of information someone can be actively thinking about at any one time. The brain can handle only a certain amount of information at once, so if half its capacity is being used for anxiety and rumination, it can't be used for learning or remembering. It's being wasted. Getting rid of anxiety opens up more space in the brain to work on the task at hand."

Convincing someone not to worry isn't an easy task, but worry goes hand-in-hand with physical tension, Dr. Yesavage says. "Ease the physical tension and the mind follows."

Calming music, deep breathing exercises, meditation, yoga, biofeedback, progressive relaxation training—whatever your

---

A Happy Side to Memory Loss?

Can there be anything *positive* about memory loss?

Yes, says Nancy L. Mergler, Ph.D., of the department of psychology at the University of Oklahoma, Norman. She theorizes that nature has a purpose for elders who are better at recalling long-ago events than what happened yesterday: Their role in the survival of the species is that of transmitters of information to younger generations. A study conducted by Dr. Mergler and Michael D. Goldstein, of Washington College, Maryland, tested the hypothesis that a society's elders are better storytellers, that a young audience will retain more of a particular story if it is read by a person of advanced age. Specifically, the study compared two storytellers in their early twenties, two in their forties, and two aged 67 and 82. The audience of 144 college undergraduates listened to recordings of stories read by a member of one group or another and then were asked to repeat verbatim what they could remember. As expected, the subjects recalled more of stories read by the older group; this suggests that, as we age, we acquire various story-telling skills that have to do with speech patterns. In subsequent studies, Dr. Mergler and Goldstein will investigate the story-telling ability of elders who spin their own yarns rather than reading a prepared script.

---

own personal antidote to anxiety may be, just keep in mind that worrying about forgetting is like scratching poison ivy. You'll only make matters worse.

Our Moody Filing Cabinets

When we are happy, our memories tend to record positive, pleasant events; when sad, we are apt to remember any unpleasantness that comes our way. Because memory tends to be selective in this way, our moods tend to perpetuate themselves, and it can be hard to dig ourselves out of a depression. Psychologists call this effect "mood congruity." Many of us have learned to break a chain of negative thoughts by seeking a diversion—seeing a film or taking a trip, for example.

A related phenomenon is "state dependency": We are more apt to recall a memory when we are in the same state of mind as when we recorded it. This may explain why we have trouble recalling both dreams from the night before and also memories stored when we were babies. Similarly, some murderers appear to have no recall of the act they performed in a blinding anger; and people who drink to excess may recall few of the indiscreet comments they let fly while inebriated at a party.

What is the practical impact of these findings and theories? Simply that the memory is wonderfully complex, more so than is suggested when it is referred to as a file drawer or computer. This complexity is responsible for occasional glitches, when memories just won't come to us on demand. On the other hand, it also guarantees a richness of association, whereby we retrieve not only bits of information, but also an interwoven fabric of insight and trivia, of fantasy and hard fact. So it is that a character of French novelist Marcel Proust unlocked several novels' worth of old memories just by nibbling on a madeleine cookie dipped in lime-flower tea. Try doing *that* with a file drawer or computer.

Memory around the Clock

Your memory is not at its best all through the day. Like many other natural phenomena, it waxes and wanes on a 24-hour cycle. You'll retain more of the material you want to learn once you can identify the hours that work best for you.

This much has been discovered from recent research. But studies don't agree on just when the memory is at its sharpest. Writing in *Nature* (May 25, 1978), two British researchers reported that "burning the midnight oil" may not be the best strategy for cramming information into your brain. Timothy H. Monk and Simon Folkard, of the University of Sussex's Laboratory of Experimental Psychology, showed a training film to subjects at either 4 A.M. or 8:30 P.M., then tested their retention immediately after the screening. Those who saw the film at 4 A.M. did slightly better. But a second test, given 28 days later, produced dramatically different results: The 4 A.M. group forgot more than twice as much as those who had seen the film at 8:30 P.M. So, while you may sense that your memory is sharpest late at night, your hard-learned information may not stay in your head as long as you'd wish.

A related finding was that our level of recall is affected more by the time of day at which the information was absorbed than the time at which we attempt to remember it.

Focus Your Attention

The cause of absentmindedness is given right in the term. The mind literally is absent, and tending to other matters, when it supposedly is recording where you put your keys or what foods your spouse wants you to pick up from the market on the way home from work.

In *Absent Minded?*, authors James Reason and Klara Mycielska concur with Dr. Yesavage in describing attention as a limited resource. Some people have greater emotional loads placed on their attentiveness than others. Ongoing anxiety or depression and obsessive thoughts may leave little spare capacity to deal with life's situations. Even a mild depression can interfere with the mind's ability to absorb information. "Up to 10 percent of elderly patients thought to have dementia may make an excellent recovery with antidepressant treatment," reports physician Robert A. Wood in the *British Medical Journal* (May 12, 1984).

The persistent thoughts that divert a person's attention are called "cognitive demons," a term that has its counterpart in Eastern spiritual writings: Novice meditators are said to be distracted by stray thoughts referred to as "monkeys." In fact, therapist and memory book author Joan Minninger likens studying to a person's first attempts to meditate, in that both student and meditator are apt to be plagued by "a rush of distracting ideas, thoughts, and body sensations."

What's going on upstairs? Why can concentration be so difficult? Dr. Minninger theorizes that thinking with a tight focus is a relatively new skill for the human species. An animal in the wild must use a wide focus to scan the environment for threats, if it is to survive. Think of a songbird, sitting nervously on a branch and trying to look in all directions at once. That's the appropriate attitude when checking the yard for cats, but it wouldn't work for a person reading a difficult novel.

Poor concentration is the bane of many students, and in some professions it can be hazardous. Reason and Mycielska study the mental slips that have led to some of the worst airline and railroad tragedies. They reconstruct the moments before the crash, and note the drains on the crew's attention—emotional stress, boredom, lack of sleep, a change in daily routine. The operator of a British subway took his train right into a wall, and his face, glimpsed by a witness just seconds before impact, showed no concern whatsoever. His mind, the authors suggest, was absent.

Techniques for Better Concentration

Whether you are taxiing a plane down a runway or merely looking for your glasses, here are several ways to keep your cognitive demons on the leash. Reason and Mycielska mention meditation as a means of focusing attention. More persistent emotional stress may yield to psychotherapy. For many of us, the answer is simpler. If our lives (and desks) are disorganized, a result can be a corresponding level of mental clutter. "Create a structure for your possessions," coaches Dr. Minninger, and use it. "No structure works if you don't use it." In its survey of executives with especially good memories, *Fortune* magazine (August 28, 1978) quotes Chrysler chairman Lee Iacocca: "If you care, you remember." He starts his day by mentally ranking the things he has to accomplish in the hours ahead.

You can also take a course in organizing skills. At Workability in New York City, a four-hour course is said to increase a person's productivity with a system of keeping the business day in order. Workability's Paula Geyer likens an office worker's well-meaning efforts at straightening up the desk and files to a fifth grader with a September resolution to keep a tidy notebook.

In his book *Fat Paper: Diets for Trimming Paperwork* (McGraw-Hill, 1978), management services director Lee Grossman says that some people have a deep psychological need to surround themselves with paperwork. Drowning in a sea of paperwork actually can feel good—if you feel insecure when not constantly busy; if memos and forms compensate for a lack of true communication and organization; if the safe routines of paper-shuffling ease the anxieties of the job. Paper accumulates as naturally in a middle-aged business as middle-age spread does in a middle-aged person, writes Grossman. Controlling fat paper takes a conscious decision to do so.

The first step, suggests Grossman, is to challenge each paperwork ritual with the question, "Why?" Why is the form necessary? And why is it necessary to handle it repeatedly, or to honor it with a place in a filing cabinet? Although his book is directed to corporate managers, Grossman's tips apply to each of us who uses a desk and files, or works at home.

Memory Food

Our memory power is influenced by what we eat and drink. It also is quick to register the brain-numbing effects of alcohol, nicotine, and many drugs.

As explained in chapter 2, the brain's business is accomplished by cells firing off messages between each other. These transactions are encouraged or discouraged by the presence of brain chemicals called neurotransmitters. One transmitter, acetylcholine, is particularly involved with memory function, and others are thought to play a role as well.

This would be only so much science, with little application for you, if it weren't for a discovery made in the 1970s by researchers at MIT. They found that levels of neurotransmitters in the brain correspond to blood levels of the nutrients (called precursors) from which they are made. And precursor levels, in turn, reflect what we've been eating. A number of nutrients influence the brain's work within minutes after they've been ingested.

This is important news to anyone who wants to keep mentally sharp; it is of special importance to older people. Although relatively few of us will suffer serious memory impairment, a small decline in certain memory functions is common. The gradual loss of brain cells over the years may be partly responsible. To ensure the best performance of those billions of cells left to us, we can consciously adapt our diets and life habits to favor them.

In an area of study that is so new, it's understandable that researchers have more tantalizing leads than they do prescriptions for sharp memory. Still, enough is known to suggest which foods you may want to include in your diet and which you may want to leave alone.

The neurotransmitter most associated with memory function, acetylcholine, is made from choline, an essential amino acid that occurs in many foods, predominately eggs, liver, soybeans, cabbage, cauliflower, and a soybean product, lecithin. It is a popular nutritional supplement, and is used as an additive to improve the consistency of such foods as ice cream, mayonnaise, and margarine. (Supplements labeled as lecithin may contain other substances as well, such as inositol; read the labels before buying.)

The brains of patients suffering from the most common form of senility, Alzheimer's disease, are characteristically low in the enzyme necessary for the production of acetylcholine. The less of this enzyme that's present, the more severe the case of Alzheimer's. In a recent study at the University of Modena in Italy, Alzheimer's patients treated with choline showed significant improvement in memory and perception.

For the great majority of older people who aren't troubled by senility, there nevertheless is normally some decline in the effectiveness of acetylcholine. The reasons aren't known: The aging brain may be physically less able to use the neurotransmitter; certain chemicals in the brain that inactivate neurotransmitters may be doing too good a job; or the brain could be producing too little acetylcholine simply because the diet is deficient in choline-rich foods.

Are most older people walking cases of lecithin deficiency? Richard Wurtman, M.D., an MIT neuroendocrinologist who has done much work in this area, believes that what is considered a "normal" level of lecithin in the diet may become insufficient as people age. He suggests that "choline or lecithin may even improve memory among otherwise normal young people with relatively poor memory functions."

While stating this, Dr. Wurtman takes care to draw a distinction between taking choline as part of a meal, on one hand, and taking it as a drug—in large amounts and in pure form. It is as a drug that practitioners are likely to use choline and other precursors, he explains, because these nutrients occur in relatively small amounts in foods. He expects that physicians soon will be able to prescribe combinations of precursors to treat specific mental problems. For example, there is reason to believe that Alzheimer's disease may involve problems with the neurotransmitters catecholamine and serotonin as well as choline; this would suggest including their precursors, tyrosine and tryptophan, in a remedy.

Although neurotransmitter precursors are low in most of the foods we eat, at least this buffering effect assures us that here is a relatively safe approach to encouraging the brain's best performance.

Memory Pills

Can the memory be rejuvenated with drugs? The search for mental elixirs goes on, and from time to time, hints of success are reported in medical journals and the popular press. But none has yet been proven to be a safe cure-all.

In the 1960s and 1970s, procaine was the memory drug most often in the news. It has found wide use in Europe, but the FDA never approved it for use in the U.S. (The manufacture and prescription of procaine are legal in the state of Nevada, however.)

Procaine is a local anesthetic that was first used to stem the effects of aging and degenerative diseases by Ana Aslan, a Rumanian physician, in the early 1950s. Her formulation of the drug, labeled Gerovital, has been taken by thousands in Europe. According to the journal *Geriatrics* (April, 1982), John F. Kennedy, Marlene Dietrich, Charles de Gaulle, Somerset Maugham, Kirk Douglas, and Mao Tse Tung showed interest in it.

In the early 1970s, the *Washington Post* (March 14, 1973) referred to Dr. Aslan as a "modern-day Ponce de Leon." And in 1975, the Rumanian Tourist Office offered a "Keep Young" tour to Aslan's Institute of Geriatrics, near Bucharest, complete with tablets or injections of Gerovital. But scientists in America have faulted Dr. Aslan's research as not sufficiently rigorous to determine its real worth. Studies in the U.S. have produced a mixed verdict; some researchers found the drug effective only as an antidepressant and others detected no improvement whatsoever.

Dr. Aslan has countered that these studies were conducted with straight procaine, rather than her preparation of procaine combined with trace amounts of benzoic acid, potassium meta-bisulfate, and disodium phosphate—additives that slow the breakdown of procaine and thereby increase its potency, her argument goes. But doubts have been expressed by a group of three physicians writing a comprehensive review on procaine in the *Journal of the American Geriatrics Society*. Dr. Adrian Ostfeld, Dr. Cedric M. Smith, and Dr. Bernard A. Stotsky read 285 articles and books in nine languages, and they conclude that the drug's apparent benefit to older people comes through its antidepressant effect, rather than by acting on specific diseases of aging. Someone taking Gerovital may *feel* rejuvenated, but this could be because a number of old-age symptoms are aggravated by depression.

In 1981, the news concerned vasopressin, a drug prescribed to encourage the kidneys to retain water and to constrict blood vessels (not available in Great Britain). Researchers in the Netherlands and at the National Institute of Mental Health reported that it yielded significantly improved performances on memory tests by both college students and older people.

So why hasn't vasopressin become a household word? First of all, the drug can be dangerous because of its effects on the kidneys and circulatory system. One form of the drug is reported to restrict its power to the memory, but even this new and improved version will have to go through years of testing before it can be prescribed.

Hyperoxygenation Hype?

Pure oxygen, administered through a mask, has been used in an attempt to improve the memories of older people. Some hospitals have installed "hyperbaric oxygen chambers," following their development in the 1960s by Eleanor Jacobs, a psychologist at Buffalo Veterans Administration Hospital. But subsequent studies by the National Institute of Mental Health debunked hyperoxygenation, and found that patients felt better after a treatment simply because they were impressed by the chamber. In other words, improvements were apparently traceable to the placebo effect.

A third drug is Hydergine, prescribed to counteract the effects of aging on the brain and to revive the memory in particular. It may work by enhancing the transmission of neurotransmitters. In his evaluation of Hydergine in *The Complete Guide to Anti-Aging Nutrients*, Dr. Sheldon Saul Hendler calls the drug "a very promising substance that may eventually be shown to have a protective role against dementia." But he cautions that researchers still do not know enough about its long-term effects or its value in preventing a mental decline. Currently, the drug is available by prescription only.

Alcohol

Alcohol can be unfriendly to memory function. Predictably, its memory-pickling effect is most pronounced in heavy drinkers. In fact, all chronic alcoholics, no matter what their age, can look forward to profound deficits in both memory and learning. Less well known is the fact that even social drinkers may be tampering with their short-term memory.

Apparently, drinking interferes with storage—that is, the brain's ability to process new information and commit it to memory. On the other hand, a person under the influence may not be hindered in recalling memories that were stored when sober. So, your ability to retrieve facts while playing Trivial Pursuit won't necessarily be impaired if you sip alcoholic drinks between turns.

Drinking and studying don't mix well, because alcohol can sabotage your efforts to store new information. Alcohol causes you to lay down "weaker traces" of memory, suggest researchers Isabel Birnbaum and Elizabeth Parker in *Alcohol and Human Memory*.

Chronic alcoholism may speed up the decline in mental performance that normally accompanies aging. That's the theory put forth by Christopher Ryan, Ph.D., and Nelson Butters, Ph.D., in *Alcoholism: Clinical and Experimental Research* (July, 1980). From their work, they found "the scores earned by 34- to 49-year-old alcoholics on our verbal tests do not differ statistically from those of 50- to 59-year-old controls. Likewise, the scores of 50- to 59-year-old alcoholic subjects are indistinguishable from those earned by 60- to 65-year-old nonalcoholics." As a cause of progressive dementia, alcoholism ranks the fourth most common.

That's chilling evidence for habitual drinkers. But what about the great majority of drinkers who take their alcohol in moderate, occasional doses? In the *Journal of Studies on Alcohol* (January, 1980), a summary of research on social drinking states that "moderate doses of alcohol impair such cognitive processes as abstracting ability, information processing, and, in particular, memory." What's more, these cognitive abilities show deficits even when social drinkers are tested sober. Perhaps you yourself have witnessed this problem when trying to remember conversations from a party the night before.

This sobering news is tempered somewhat by evidence that the brain can forgive as well as forget. According to Elizabeth Loftus, alcohol's impairment of memory "largely disappears if and when the person stops drinking. Alcoholics who were tested four to five weeks after starting treatment performed remarkably well on memory tests."

Not everyone is equally susceptible to alcohol's effects on

Smoke Damage

Apparently, the nicotine in cigarette smoke interferes with memory, according to researchers at UCLA. They measured the verbal recall performance of smokers after smoking either filtered or nicotine-free cigarettes. When both groups were tested again two days later, the inferior performance of those who smoked the nicotine cigarettes led the researchers to conclude that their "short-term memory was significantly hindered." Nicotine was also found to sabotage the memory in a study at the University of Edinburgh, Scotland, this one comparing 37 smokers with 37 nonsmokers. Subjects were tested on their recall of the names of 12 people shown in photographs. Non-smokers correctly remembered a mean of nearly 9 out of 12, while smokers (they averaged a pack a day) could not quite come up with 7.

the brain. That's the finding of Charles Golden, Ph.D., professor of medical psychology at the University of Nebraska, Omaha. Certain individuals suffer damage "much faster and at lower levels of alcohol than most people," he says. "It's not so much the amount of alcohol that matters, it's an individual's reaction to it." People who seem to overreact to even small amounts of alcohol—who experience marked personality changes or black-outs or confusion—might consider themselves especially susceptible, Dr. Golden says.

Curiously, women and men are not affected equally by alcohol. The research of Marilyn K. Jones and Ben Morgan Jones, reported in the *Journal of Studies on Alcohol*, suggests that relatively light drinking has more impact on the short-term memory of women than on that of men. As for heavy drinking, alcoholic women show impaired verbal and spatial cognitive ability, while alcoholic men demonstrate only spatial difficulties.

Does the Memory Wear Out?

All too often, older people *assume* they are becoming forgetful simply because they've had a certain number of birthdays. They fall prey to a damaging cultural stereotype—the doddering "golden-ager" who has a memory like a sieve, whose mind is as stiff and inflexible as an arthritic joint. They may fear the gradual slide into senility as being inevitable.

These assumptions had gone largely unchallenged until a few years ago, when research on aging brought about a new appreciation for the memory's resilience throughout life. Consider the following findings:

- Although a modest impairment of some memory functions is a normal part of aging, most of us can expect to enjoy our good memories well into old age. Memory declines are both smaller and occur later in life than previously believed, according to Judith Ford, Ph.D., and Walton T. Roth, M.D., in the journal *Geriatrics* (September, 1977).
- Brain cells do die in great numbers, as is popularly believed. But even at a clip of 50,000 to 100,000 neurons a day (as is often quoted), we stand to lose only 1 billion of our 15 billion cells by age 70.
- Relatively few older people become truly senile. Many apparent cases of senility can be traced to poor diet, drug reactions, confusion after hospitalization, low self-esteem, and society's indifference to the elderly. All of these causes are reversible.
- Memory is a tool that becomes sharper with use. You can't wear it out or use it up. As we grow older, we can consciously take on new challenges for the purpose of keeping our memories fit.

We live in a society that expects less from its older members. "Our conception of old age is a bad habit," writes anthropologist Ashley Montague in *Growing Older*. He refers to the segregation between age groups in our society as "agism," and says that physicians are not immune from it; they may assume a case of untreatable memory loss when the true problem lies elsewhere. "Doctors do themselves and their patients an injustice if they believe that a failing memory is a sign of old age," agrees Peter H. Millard, professor of geriatric medicine at St. George's Hospital Medical School in London. In the *British Medical Journal* (October 27, 1984), he asks, "In examining the elderly may we not find what we expect to find? Because we see old age as a problem, do we report only negative findings?"

The very fear of forgetting can cause older people to fumble for names and telephone numbers. It also sends many of them to the Bornstein School of Memory Training in Los Angeles. "Older people anticipate a memory loss," explains Arthur Bornstein; he says that a large part of his job is restoring their confidence.

In an article on memory loss in the *Lancet*, British physician Robert A. Wood suggests that the medical profession should reassure middle-aged and older patients that forgetting an occasional name is not an early indication of senility; he refers to this common occurrence as "benign forgetfulness."

Because anxiety numbs the memory, it makes little sense for older people to worry about memory loss. Behavioral psychologist and author B. F. Skinner (himself now entering his eighties) has found that a "calm acceptance" of occasional memory lapses can go a long way toward allowing elusive memories to surface. "Graceful ways of explaining your [memory] failure may help," he said in an address before a convention of the American Psychological Association. Embarrassed by forgetting the name of an acquaintance? "Flatter your listener by saying that you have noticed that the more important the person, the easier it is to forget the name."

Another strategy proposed by Dr. Skinner is "good intellectual self-management." The examples he gives are common-sense suggestions that anyone, at any age, might follow. When you hear that rain is expected, immediately hook an umbrella over the knob of the front door so that you can't very well leave home without it. To capture creative ideas that visit you in the middle of the night, keep a note pad or tape recorder by the bed. ("The problem in old age is not so much how to have ideas as how to have them when you can use them.") A pocket notebook can "maximize one's intellectual output" by receiving ideas, names, and numbers as they come up and by enabling them to be retrieved easily. "In place of memories," advises Dr. Skinner, "memorandums." (Note-taking is a useful habit that older people tend to lose, says Penn State gerontologist Nancy J. Treat.) To avoid losing your train of thought when speaking, continues Dr. Skinner, keep sentences short and to the point, and beware of digressions that may take you far from your original point. And when writing, try using an outline to guard against inconsistencies and repetition. An ongoing index may help you to keep track of your material as you build it into a paper or chapter or long letter.

Is It Really Senility?

A diagnosis of senile dementia—or the mental disability of old age—can land a person in an institution. So can a misdiagnosis, and this is the tragic fate of an alarming number of older people whose confusion and memory loss can actually be traced to drugs, malnutrition, depression, anemia, pneumonia, hormone imbalance, dehydration, hypothyroidism, hypoglycemia, or vitamin B_{12} deficiency. Older people are prone to a mistaken diagnosis of senile dementia because doctors "expect old people to dement," says Leslie G. Kiloh, professor of psychiatry at the University of New South Wales, Australia. In the *Medical Journal of Australia*, he mentions studies that report 5 to 10 percent of patients referred to hospitals with diagnoses of "incurable dementia" were found to be treatable, and another 5 to 10 percent turned out not to be demented at all. In the U.S., from 15 to 30 percent of Alzheimer's diagnoses may be mistaken, according to Margaret M. Heckler, U.S. Secretary of Health and Human Services. And that is a serious mistake. Once a person is labeled a victim of Alzheimer's, treatment ceases; the disease is currently incurable. At a 1985 conference on Alzheimer's, several experts agreed that the disease had become a "garbage pail" diagnosis into which unknown problems are dumped.

Depression is one of the most common causes of pseudo-senility. Depressed people tend to have poor concentration, show little interest in their surroundings, and be untidy in appearance—all of which may contribute to a misdiagnosis. If the black moods lead to heavy drinking, then alcohol may contribute its own memory deficits. A person who is depressed rather than senile may give telltale signs: awareness of the disability, an up-and-down history of ability to perform, and an equal impairment of remote and recent memory.

A number of drugs undermine the memory. Unfortunately, the aged are not only the age group most often affected—they take more kinds of drugs than other population groups—but also the group least able to afford this memory loss. The more drugs a person takes, the greater the possibility for unhappy interactions. On top of this, an older person may have kidneys and a liver that are less efficient in clearing drugs from the body. Further, a not-so-obvious toll of subclinical malnutrition in many older people is that some medications will act more potently. Penicillin takes longer to leave the body, for example. On the other hand, the absorption of tetracycline is decreased in a malnourished person.

The list of memory-damaging drugs is "endless," according to Dr. Millard. "Indeed, it is surprising that the medicated aged pass any mental tests at all." He suggests to physicians that if a patient has loss of memory, the first question should be, "Is anything that I am prescribing causing it?" And in *Total Recall,* Dr. Minninger suggests that you yourself can check on side effects of a drug if you suspect it is affecting your memory: Ask your doctor; read the literature that came with the product; or go straight to the library and consult pharmacological text books.

Drugs that may contribute to loss of memory include barbiturates and other sedatives, benzodiasepines, tricyclic antidepressants, antihistamines, certain anticonvulsants, diuretics, and tranquilizers—Valium in particular. Mohamed Ghoneim, professor of anesthesia at the University of Iowa, advises physicians to use caution in prescribing Valium to students about to take examinations. Although volunteers in a study gradually developed a degree of tolerance to this popularly prescribed drug, their performance on recall tests did not come back up to pre-Valium levels.

And what should you do if you suspect a drug of impinging upon your memory? Dr. Wood says the treatment may be as simple as cutting down on the dosage, switching to another drug, or discontinuing the drug altogether—as your doctor advises, of course.

Alzheimer's and Senile Dementia

In this book of predominantly good news about the brain and its amazing capabilities, the next few pages will stand out as particularly gloomy. Alzheimer's disease and other, less-known forms of senile dementia involve a progressive degeneration of the brain. The impairment begins as forgetfulness and leads to complete disablement and death from related complications. The cause is not presently known; nor is there a cure.

An important point that tends to be overlooked is that these are *diseases*, and not merely symptoms of aging. Senility is not an inevitable part of old age. The confusion arises for a couple of reasons. First, because Alzheimer's does in fact become more prevalent in later years, it is often thought of as an "old person's disease." Second, it so happens that the first symptom of Alzheimer's—occasional forgetfulness—is common among healthy older people.

Alzheimer's disease was discovered in 1907 by Alois Alzheimer, a German neurologist. Although the disease can affect people in their forties and fifties, it does not do so frequently. Generally, the earlier the age at which Alzheimer's occurs, the more severe its symptoms and the quicker its development. The disease is thought to affect over 750,000 people in Great Britain. Of this total 25 percent of sufferers are aged between 45 and 54, 72 percent of them are aged between 54 and 65 and 2.3 percent of them are aged between 65 and 69. Sufferers typically become seriously demented from three to ten years after the onset of symptoms.

Alzheimer's is responsible for half the 1.3 million patients in America's nursing homes. It is the fourth leading cause of death in the U.S., according to a Senate report. Magnifying concern over the disease is the fact that the fastest growing segment of the population is the U.S. is the elderly population.

The disease characteristically passes through several progressive stages of impairment, outlined in *Clinical Psychiatry News* (February, 1985):

1. No noticeable symptoms
2. Minor forgetfulness
3. Trouble in performing a job
4. Trouble in balancing the chequebook, planning a dinner party
5. Can get dressed, but picks out appropriate clothes with difficulty; denial of symptoms
6. Cannot get dressed or bathe alone; incontinence; severe memory problems (may not remember name of spouse at some times)
7. Progressive loss of ability to speak, walk, sit up
8. Coma and death

Who is most at risk? Reporting in the *Journal of the American Geriatrics Society* (October, 1982), researchers at the University of Wisconsin and the University of Saskatchewan suggest that children born of older mothers may be more inclined to get the disease later in life; another theory is that some people are genetically predisposed.

The brains of Alzheimer's victims reveal physical changes that offer some clues to the disease's origin. Significant numbers of brain cells are lost, and the brain's shrinkage is pronounced. Levels of acetylcholine are lower than normal, suggesting that this neurotransmitter might be involved. Other possible explanations include a reduced blood flow to the brain, a virus, nutritional deficiencies, and toxins in the environment.

The toxin most often implicated is aluminum, a metal that until rather recently was assumed to be benign. It finds its way into the body by a number of means that people may not be conscious of—from aluminium cooking and drinking vessels, aluminium salts in baking powder, antacids, and even through the skin from antiperspirants. Researchers at the Brain Bio Center in Princeton, New Jersey, note that people complaining of memory loss have a significantly higher mean blood aluminium level. And in the brains of Alzheimer's patients, certain regions contain high levels of aluminium. Blood aluminium levels can be reduced through supplements of other minerals—zinc, manganese, and magnesium, according to the Brain Bio Center researchers.

But even if the metal is a neurotoxin that interferes with mental functions, this does not constitute a solid case against the metal. Do high levels of aluminium bring on Alzheimer's, or is the metal merely absorbed by the "neurofibrillary tangles" that are a characteristic formation of the disease? Richard Wurtman, M.D., a neuroendocrinologist at MIT, suggests that aluminium may only emphasize symptoms that are already caused by an as-yet-to-be-identified factor.

Conflicting with the theory that Alzheimer's is nutritionally caused is a study described in the *Journal of the American Geriatrics Society* (October, 1984). Researchers found no significant difference between the blood levels of 12 vitamins in 55 Alzheimer's patients and those in 58 control subjects. The conclusion was that "conventional vitamin malnutrition did not seem to contribute to the disability."

As for the theory proposing reduced blood flow as the cause, evidence exists that certain brain regions of Alzheimer's patients pick up 30 percent less oxygen and 30 to 50 percent less glucose from the blood than do the brains of older people who aren't afflicted.

Dr. Wurtman says that the most promising lead in sleuthing the cause of Alzheimer's disease is the inability of some brains to produce sufficient acetylcholine, due to a loss of the nerve terminals that release this neurotransmitter. An abnormality here, says Dr. Wurtman, "seems to many of us to be the clue most likely to eventually point to the cause of Alzheimer's disease."

The next step is to find a way to bring the acetylcholine levels back up. One strategy would be to administer a drug that inhibits the breakdown of acetylcholine by the brain's chemicals; a problem here is that the drug also would affect areas of the brain that are not troubled. A second possibility is to stimulate the release of acetylcholine in the brain with a drug. Third, more of the neurotransmitter's precursor could be made available to the brain.

Several medical journal articles discuss accomplishing this by giving patients supplemental lecithin. But in an article in *Scientific American* (January, 1985), Dr. Wurtman says that there has only been one "long-term, carefully controlled study" on the effect of giving lecithin to Alzheimer's patients, and the findings are not without serious questions. Raymond Levy, of the University of London Faculty of Medicine, observed improved behavior in 8 of 24 Alzheimer's patients given puri-fied lecithin. The qualification is this: The 8 were an average of 79 years old, compared to 69 years for those who did not show an improvement; and, as noted earlier in this chapter, young Alzheimer's sufferers are thought to contract a more serious case of the disease.

When All Else Fails, Forget It

Sometimes, forgetfulness is more frustrating than it is prob-lematic. Forgetting may be okay, says Dr. Minninger in *Total Recall,* if it doesn't interfere with your life or upset others. Invest in extra sets of keys and hide them everywhere; plan on paying for the occasional missed appointment or cheque drawn on an empty account.

Absentmindedness can be a lovable trait, and it does seem to go hand in hand with creativity. Every workplace has its detail people and its creative people. If you find yourself in the latter party, take solace in the example of Albert Einstein, the genius who, when working at Princeton University, once had to call the switchboard because he forgot where he lived. He would have called home but, as the story has it, the number was unlisted and he couldn't remember that, either.

7

Learn to Be
More Creative

Not everyone would agree with the argument in this chapter that you can increase your creative ability. Isn't creativity an innate talent, something that a person either has or hasn't, like blue eyes or the inability to comfortably digest radishes? We tend to think of it as an exotic power that *other* people possess—artists, designers, composers, scientists, or perhaps a friend who is always coming up with clever new ways to dress, decorate, and entertain.

Creativity is shrouded in myth and modern-day folklore. We find it no less mysterious than sex appeal or charisma. No wonder we can't see it for what it really is: a mental capacity, much like memory or concentration, that can be developed at any age, and one that depends on an investment of patience and work. Paul Joseph Burgett, dean of students at the Eastman School of Music, blasts the myths that "creativity is fashioned mysteriously out of nothingness," that it is "properly the domain of a privileged few."

So then, just what is creativity? Put most simply, it is the capacity for making something new. We all had plenty of it when we were very young. Being creative means exploring the unknown, and for infants, exploring is a survival skill—the only way they can learn about the world. Young people remain open, trusting, unselfconscious, and playful. This you may know, even if you can't recall scenes from your own childhood, by watching kids at the beach. The props are simple. Just sand, water, scraps of shell. But the variations are infinite.

So, what happens to us and our bountiful creativity when we grow up? Why do our curiosity, playfulness, and sense of wonder all seem to dry up? If we answer these questions, we may get some insight into how we can regain the ability to combine things and ideas in new ways.

We learn early that our creative explorations into the unknown may not be acceptable to those around us. Crying is an example. A child soon learns to check this simple form of expression. Later, teachers prune back creative responses in order to make a child more manageable, and that seems reasonable enough, in a room with 30 children exploring in 30 different directions.

But some researchers and educators believe we've gone too far in coaxing standardized behavior from our kids. When classes are geared toward producing one correct answer, creativity is squeezed out of education. Creativity defies measurement, says George S. Welsh, Ph.D., who has studied ways of detecting it at North Carolina's Institute for Research in Social Science. All children are tested for their mental ability, but only intelligence and certain specific attitudes are detected, not creativity. So it is that the especially creative child may go unnoticed, and is not likely to receive special attention. On the contrary, creative behavior may earn a child the teacher's disapproval, for not following instructions, for not coloring within the lines, for making a purple tree, for making the class laugh. After a few years of this, most children learn all too well to behave within the limits of their teachers' and parents' expectations.

Throughout history, creative thinkers have earned the fear and hate of others. Paul Burgett gives as examples the young boy who plays the violin and "is labeled 'queer' by his peers"; and the young woman who is "practicing the carpenter's trade [and] is branded 'unfeminine' by the culture."

The culture in the U.S. may be particularly inhospitable to creative expression by individuals. Italian author Silvo Arieti writes in *Creativity* (Basic Books, 1976) that America focuses instead on productivity and efficiency.

Creative Resuscitation

Fortunately for us veterans of schooling and parental influence, creativity can rebound later in life. Each of us has the opportunity to act creatively dozens of times a day. Even taking a different way home from work counts as creative, says Burgett. We are creative whenever we decide to open ourselves to the unknown—and that may only mean taking a left onto a side street rather than sticking to the usual homeward route.

Of course, creativity on this level may not be in the same league as painting the ceiling of the Sistine Chapel or discovering penicillin. Such feats are one rung above the everyday variety of creativity, according to psychologist Abraham H. Maslow in *The Farther Reaches of Human Nature* (Viking, 1971). Still higher on the creative ladder is the magical moment in which the creative person "loses his past and his future and lives only in the moment," as Maslow describes it. "He is all there, totally immersed, fascinated and absorbed in the present."

And that's not all. The inventory of emotions coursing through the person in the throes of creation may include "bliss, ecstasy, rapture, exaltation," and perhaps you can add a few from your own forays into the unknown. "At such moments," says Maslow, "we humans are at our most mature and evolved," and what's more, also our most *healthy*, in the broad sense of the term.

What could be more wonderful? And yet few of us explore these moments, even though we are adults and no longer under the thumb of parents and teachers. That's because, even for us adults, life is simpler and safer if we *don't* take a chance on that side street on the way home. Or, if we don't follow through on an idea for a small business, or if we don't take seriously the half-finished novel that sits at the back of the sock drawer, or if we don't risk the stares that wearing a somewhat outrageous paisley blouse might attract.

"Bridging the gap between the known and the unknown poses real difficulties for most human beings," says Burgett. Studies of how to be creative eventually get down to a discussion of courage: A person must summon up courage in order to take those chances that creativity always involves.

Burgett writes, "Courage is needed to reverse the process of

Learn to Duck Before Your Ideas Are Shot At

To come up with new ideas is to invite criticism. And criticism can ultimately cause us to abandon our fondest projects. Vincent Ryan Ruggiero, professor at the State University of New York, thinks it helps to anticipate such responses. First, we'll be less apt to be discouraged when we hear them; second, we may choose to rework aspects of our ideas that are most likely to trigger these criticisms. Here is Ruggiero's list, taken from his guide, *The Art of Thinking* (Harper & Row, 1984).

The solution is:
- impractical
- too expensive
- illegal
- immoral
- inefficient
- unworkable
- disruptive of existing procedures
- unaesthetic
- too radical
- unappealing to others
- prejudiced against one side of a dispute

not being creative and to begin to reclaim the natural curiosity all humans possess at birth." We can feel real fear before a blank canvas or a typewriter, and these are only the most obvious examples: Everyday living also demands that we be flexible and experimental. Maslow says that a society requires "people who don't need to staticize the world, who don't need to freeze it and to make it stable, who are able confidently to face tomorrow not knowing what's going to come, with confidence enough in [themselves] that [they] will be able to improvise in that situation which has never existed before."

It may feel risky to try out original ideas when you're convinced that everyone's ready to pounce on them. Maslow writes, "Others may be upset by your originality because creativity means change, and change is threatening to people who take comfort in the status quo."

It also takes courage to turn our backs on another critical audience—ourselves. Many people are held back by an internal monitor that constantly appraises their work: "That drawing is a piece of childish garbage. You're too old to learn to sketch portraits."

So much for the hang-ups which keep us from being creative. What can we do to overcome them? Later in this chapter we'll suggest many ways to make our minds more limber, to silence the critical voices inside, to become not quite so sensitive to the critical voices around us.

Creativity Takes Youthful Thinking, Not Youth

We learn how *not* to create in our first years at school. Children are shown a model—a witch at Halloween, a fat Santa at Christmas, and so on—and are expected to reproduce it. In this way, successful students become dependent on the opinion of others when painting and writing. They even adopt stereotyped responses to the books they read and the art they see. In the *Journal of Learning Skills* (Winter, 1983), University of Vermont professor Karen Wiley Sandler describes ways to unlearn this noncreative behavior. When reading a poem, she advises, don't focus right away on meter, rhyme, and form.

These matters of structure are what we concentrate on in school, but they may make us feel remote from the work. Instead, try to identify the artist's feelings as you read, and relate these emotions to your own life if you can. Dr. Sandler asks students to keep journals in which they write their personal reactions to the literature they read. This exercise helps them to wean themselves from trying to come up with the "correct" response when reading. It helps return reading to the intimate experience it should be.

Television is another apparent threat to creativity, and recent research suggests it may deserve its nickname "the boob tube." Conventional television programming is popularly believed to offer little stimulation for the mind, and at least two studies have attempted to judge TV's impact on the creativity of school-aged children.

In one experiment, the young subjects were asked to complete an unfinished story that they either watched on TV or listened to over a speaker. Researcher Dorathea Farrar-Hartman, Ph.D., notes the "consistent finding that story completions were more imaginative following radio presentations than following television presentations."

In the second study, 102 children between the ages of 10 and 14 were given a questionnaire to determine the amount of hours they logged watching TV, reading books, and in other after-school activities. They also took Torrance's Tests of Creative Thinking, and were graded on a creative writing assignment. Of the influences looked at in this study, hours of TV watching was the best predictor of results on the creativity tests and creative writing assignment—the more hours in front of the set, the lower the creativity ratings. (Interestingly, the level of the parents' education was the variable *least* related to creativity ratings.) What was the favorite activity of those scoring high on creativity? Being with friends, found Catherine Louise Peirce, Ph.D. Among those scoring lowest, watching television was their chosen way of spending time.

Whatever the causes, it is popularly accepted that we become less creative as we age. Studies do confirm that older people may be less flexible in their handling of a project. But they may compensate for this through their use of what is called "crystallized intelligence," or the knowledge they have accumulated through life. This is a different sort of mental resource than "fluid intelligence," which describes the fluency with which a person organizes new material in the mind. A study on the changing nature of creativity throughout life, published in *Educational Gerontology* (March/April, 1982), looks at the ways in which younger and older subjects went about a creative writing assignment. The pieces were rated for creativity by three English professors on such criteria as picturesqueness, vividness, original plot and setting, and humor.

The younger subjects outperformed the older ones, generally (although the oldest of them, a woman of 83, got the second-highest creativity score of the 61 subjects, whose ages ranged from 20 on up). The researchers suggest that this is because ideas and words come more slowly to older people, and because when writing they rely more on stored knowledge than on fabricating novel twists and situations. The researchers point out that a person's level of motivation was related to how well he or she performed, and they suggest that older people can keep their creativity alive as long as they keep their interest alive; they mention a class designed to accomplish this by encouraging older people to draw on their fund of past experiences.

An often-cited study of age and mental output is H. C. Lehman's *Age and Achievement*, published in the 1950s. Lehman calculated the ages at which the best-known people in a number of arts and sciences produced their work. He found that in most fields the ages for peak production were the late twenties and early thirties; typically, the best efforts were made somewhat earlier still. Exceptions are composing, which revealed a pattern of a sustained level of output to the age of 70, and writing, with a fairly consistent output throughout life (although the single best book rarely came along after the middle thirties).

Lehman's studies of peak creativity give only part of the picture. They suggest that highly creative people make their most significant achievements in their thirties. But this does not describe how a person's creativity is apt to ebb and flow over a lifetime.

A study of 111 California schoolteachers between the ages of 20 and 83 attempted to establish the typical lifelong pattern. The Barron-Welsh Art Scale showed a significant sag in creativity starting at 25 or so, while the Guilford Tests of Divergent Thinking put the turning point in the thirties.

But what about people who continue to draw repeatedly on their creative stores over the years? Couldn't they be expected to stay more creative longer, just as other capacities—physical and mental—are kept in tune through frequent use?

This was the hypothesis of a recent study by Carrie W. Crosson and Elizabeth A. Robertson-Tchabo at the University of Maryland. They gave the Barron-Welsh test to two groups of women with a broad range of ages: The "creative" group was composed of 271 visual artists and writers from the Washington, D.C., area; and 76 well-educated students, none of whom was a professional artist, made up the control group.

Among the artists and writers, the researchers found no significant decline in creativity over the years. The controls, however, did display a significant decrease in creativity with greater age. From these data it appears that creativity can be maintained throughout life, if this capability remains particularly important to the person. For others, however, creative ability is apt to wither with disuse. And the period in life in which creativity is most likely to take a beating is the middle years.

A study in the *International Journal of Behavioral Development* (March, 1985) tested for creativity in 150 people in three age groups (25-to-35 being the "young" group, 45-to-55 the "middle-aged," and 65-to-75 the "old" group). The researchers found that the greatest differences in fluency, flexibility, and originality occurred between the young and middle-aged groups. Much smaller differences were noted between the middle-aged and older groups.

Apparently, something originality-threatening happens to many of us on the way to middle age. What could it be? The researchers mention the demands of earning a wage, keeping up a home, and raising children. "None of this will set the stage for the time and concentration that the creative processes demand," concludes the study.

The Creative Personality

Why do people even bother creating? There's a pretty discouraging theory and then there's a happier one.

The pessimist's explanation is that we create only when driven to do so by the dark, semiconscious forces within us—guilt, anxiety, aggression, hostility, and so on. Certainly some novels and paintings strike us as being products of tortured self-expression. In Vincent Van Gogh's later paintings, for example, pigment is applied in vigorous (you might say "tortured") strokes of palette knife and brush. These strokes have been cited as evidence of the artist's episodes of mental anguish.

Artists and writers themselves have suggested a link between their level of production and emotional fragility. Writer May Sarton finds that when a blue mood passes, her work comes harder, not easier. "With the return of cheerfulness I feel a sense of loss," she writes in *Journal of a Solitude* (Norton, 1973). "I am more 'normal' again, no longer that fountain of tears and intense feeling that I have been for months. Balance is achieved, or nearly. But at what price? . . . I have worked all week on a sonnet—hundreds of drafts—but it will *not* come out."

A similar message comes out in a letter Van Gogh wrote to his brother, Theo, after Theo chided him for not minding his diet. The artist responded that he purposefully fueled himself on coffee, bread, and cheap wine in order to "maintain the clear yellow light" of emotional intensity which enabled him to paint in his marathon fashion. Like Sarton, he felt that to be happy and healthy is to lose the edge necessary to create at one's peak.

Psychologist Rollo May doesn't buy the theory that people are moved to create only to compensate for some inner weakness. Although he admits that there is no shortage of painters and writers who had well-known problems with depression, alcoholism, and stormy relationships, he writes in *The Courage to Create* (Norton, 1975) that "this does not necessarily mean that creativity is the *product* of the neurosis." He would agree with Maslow's conviction that the creative process is the expression of people "in the act of actualizing themselves," and reaching "the highest degree of emotional health.... For the time being," says Maslow, "we are courageous and confident, unafraid, unanxious, unneurotic, not sick."

Scientist and author Jacob Bronowski suggests that a person is stimulated to create (in either the arts or sciences) by the discovery of connections between things—a sense of order that appears within the chaos of the universe. When harmony occurs within a person's body, it is described as physical health; and harmony between a person and the world is described as psychological health.

How else could you explain the genesis of works that seem to celebrate life—for example, the enormous, lyrical paper cutouts of Matisse's last years? The man was confined to a wheelchair and needed the help of an assistant to prepare these works, and yet in the colors and organic forms we can sense that a long and full life was coming to fruition for Matisse.

Intelligence and Creativity

Do you have to be smart in order to be creative? George Welsh, Ph.D., the University of North Carolina professor who devised a test for creativity, says that only a normal IQ is necessary. John R. Hayes, of the psychology department at Carnegie-Mellon University, agrees. Although evidence indicates that especially creative people have above-average intelligence, he believes "there is a certain minimum IQ required for creativity, after which IQ doesn't matter." Perhaps people with less-than-average intelligence find fewer opportunities for working creatively. Hayes concludes that you shouldn't let IQ worries get in the way of anything you want to write, paint, design, or dream up. You may be able to take encouragement from the guess of modern-day psychologists that the painter Rembrandt's IQ was no more than 110. Intelligence and creative talent are two different things, according to the theory of art historian Max Friedlander. He has called Van Gogh a "genius without talent," a man whose perseverance was such that he was not held back by a late start in drawing and painting, or by a less-than-awesome arsenal of natural gifts.

It's well known that Albert Einstein was something of a

What Makes an Idea-Person?

Original, mould-breaking ideas are more apt to occur to some of us than others. Luckily, any family, company, or country needs to complement its idea-people with implementers—those who can take an idea and put it into action. Here are lists of characteristics that have been used to describe both sorts of people. Of course, any individual would include a mix of these qualities.

Idea-person	Implementer
Flexible, spontaneous, non-judgmental; unconventional	Thorough and dependable
Trusts intuition, does not necessarily proceed from one logical step to another; takes advantage of chance and accident	Thinks in progression of logical steps; uncomfortable with uncertainty
Undisciplined, scattered in attention, not well organized	Has the drive and single-mindedness to see the project through
More interested in coming up with ideas than in implementing them	Is content to set to work on a less-than-brilliant idea; more practical than idealistic
Restless with the plodding pace of school or job; may not learn necessary skills (consequently, not rewarded with good grades or promotions)	Has the technical knowledge needed to get the job done (apt to be rewarded at school or on job)

failure in school. In *The Art of Thinking* (Harper & Row, 1984), Vincent Ryan Ruggiero tells that the physicist had to do an extra year of high school work before the Zurich Polytechnic School would admit him, and once there he did such lukewarm work that the school would not recommend him for a job. When he did finally land a job as a boarding school tutor, he was fired. And so on. His problems continued even when his work was undeniably good—he offered his theory of relativity as his doctoral dissertation and it was rejected. The moral of such tales (they are told of Edison as well) is that you shouldn't be too quick to conclude that you don't have the smarts to be creative.

Is One Sex More Creative than the Other?

What do you think? Popular opinion is that both sexes have their particular mental aptitudes. Studies of school-age boys and girls lend some support to this belief. About the time of junior high school, boys tend to score better on tests of spatial visualization, a measure of the ability to mentally rotate objects. Girls, on the other hand, tend to do better on tests of verbal ability.

One explanation for these sex differences has been brain development. Boys have a more highly developed right brain, according to this theory, and girls a more highly developed left brain. But some researchers say the answer lies not in the brain but in the society—the classroom, the home, the media.

According to Sharon Churnin Nash in *Sex-Related Differences in Cognitive Functioning* (Academic Press, 1979), "there is considerable agreement that, beginning in the second grade and persisting through the twelfth grade, children perceive social-verbal and artistic skills as feminine, whereas spatial, mechanical, and athletic skills are viewed as masculine." In secondary school, noncompetitive, low-achieving females tend to see achievement as inappropriate for their sex. And women may well be held back by the scarcity of role models in less traditional fields such as mathematics and the sciences. If you haven't seen someone of your sex succeeding at a particular activity, you stand to expect less for your chances of making a go of it. In *Working It Out* (Pantheon, 1978), a book describing the lives of 23 career women, all reported that they felt the lack of role models in their fields.

In the classroom, boys and girls are apt to receive subtle reinforcement and discouragement in ways that steer them down sexually stereotyped paths. According to Carol Nagy Jacklin, in *Sex-Related Differences in Cognitive Functioning*, boys typically are criticized for being unruly, while being praised for their schoolwork; girls, in contrast, tend to be criticized for their schoolwork and praised for neatness and being quiet. When a boy fails in his work, it may be blamed on his not having applied himself, whereas a girl's failure is apt to be blamed on a lack of ability. It's not hard to see how this would cultivate in females a "learned helplessness," as it is termed. "Girls give up more easily after academic failure than boys," says Jacklin, but when the classroom is experimentally changed, this helplessness "can be eliminated."

In the *International Journal of Behavioral Development* (March, 1985), researchers Jan-Erik Ruth and James E. Birren remark that the low representation of well-known women in the arts and sciences cannot be explained by an inherent difference between the sexes. They say we should look instead at the way in which our girls and boys are brought up. "The passive conformism that traditionally has been demanded of girls is not beneficial to the development of a questioning, creative attitude. Some women are still 'imprisoned' in the role of the responsible agent for caretaking and home activities, which may not give room for the time and concentration that the creative processes demand."

Time and concentration—these two resources are invaluable to anyone who hopes to explore new paths in life. And at one time or another, most of us feel that both are in painfully short supply.

Creation Takes Time

A creative act usually begins with an initial burst of inspiration. This may be a middle-of-the-night revelation of how to streamline the office's paper flow, or a plot line for a potential best-seller that pops into your mind while jogging.

As valuable as these inspirations are, and as tricky as they may be to coax out of the brain, they're actually "a dime a dozen," says Abraham Maslow. Much tougher is the time-consuming challenge of creativity's second stage: making something of that great brainstorm.

This is where most great ideas drop into the dust along the road of inspired intentions. No doubt you have had the exasperating experience of finding that someone else just made headlines (and perhaps a fortune as well) by coming out with an idea that you had *years* ago. The difference was that while this particular someone took the time to see the idea through, you did not.

And you probably had your reasons. Stage two is littered with pitfalls, many of them having to do with time. Most obviously, great creative achievements tend to demand training or education—an apprenticeship of some sort. Is it possible for someone with no experience in art to sit down and spontaneously paint a masterpiece? If your answer is yes, then alter the question to fit your own line of expertise, whatever it may be. Could a rank novice come along and tackle your job in a radically imaginative way? Probably not. Behind almost every work of imagination is a great deal of patient work, as Thomas A. Edison impressed on us with his famous statement that a feat of genius is 99 percent perspiration and 1 percent inspiration. Or, as Maslow puts it, the second stage of creativity "relies very much on just plain hard work, on the discipline of the artist who may spend half a lifetime learning his tools, his skills, and his materials until he becomes finally ready for a full expression of what he sees. . . ."

Similarly, novelist Doris Lessing has said that the most valuable quality for an aspiring writer is perseverance. And novelist Kurt Vonnegut, Jr., says in a *Paris Review* interview that, "in a creative writing class of 20 people anywhere in this country, 6 students will be startlingly talented. Two of those might actually publish something by and by. They will be distinguished by their perseverance. . . . They won't wait passively for somebody to discover them. They will insist on being read" (*Writers at Work*, vol. 6, Viking, 1984).

Continues Maslow, "The difference between the inspiration and the final product, for example, Tolstoy's *War and*

Peace, is an awful lot of hard work, an awful lot of discipline, an awful lot of training, an awful lot of finger exercises and practices and rehearsals." And yet, the mark of a master is that he or she makes a complex task seem effortless. This is another reason we tend to overlook the long days of hard work that laid the foundation for their success.

In his book *The Complete Problem Solver* (Franklin Institute Press, 1981), Dr. Hayes looks at the lives of composers for an idea of how much time must be invested before great works flow forth. Charting the numbers of works a year produced by 76 composers over their professional lives, he finds that, on average, composers don't hit their strides until they've put in 25 years or so.

The same holds for excellence in most creative fields. It took Edison 13 years to perfect the phonograph—and he only allowed himself 4 hours of sleep a night! Hayes says that Nobel Laureate Herbert Simon spent some 100 hours a week for years in his field of economics—and that's out of a week that grants us just 168 hours. Simon may work longer hours than most, but Hayes points out that University of California professors put in an average of 60 hours on the job each week, in teaching and research.

The older we get, the more we feel the pinch of time. The first uncomfortable twinges are apt to come in mid-life. In the *International Review of Psycho-Analysis* (no. 46, 1965), Elliott Jaques says that many artists reach an impasse in their late thirties. To an older person, this sense of time as a precious quantity may seem a little premature in a person still in the fourth decade of life. But it's a common feeling, writes Jaques, especially for those who are in creative fields. Art eats up an enormous amount of time, and for the artist or would-be artist who suddenly realizes that life is not infinite, death may loom close. The resulting mid-life crisis can break them if left unresolved, says Jaques. They may drop their work or even take their lives. Or, if they come to grips with their problem, perhaps through their art, their careers may blossom. So it happened for Joseph Conrad, a sea captain who published his first novel, *Almayer's Folly,* at the age of 37.

In her study on Conrad's mid-life crisis, published in the

International Review of Psycho-Analysis (vol. 11, no. 1, 1984), Hanna Segal adds that these anxieties over death have to be met successfully. Failure to do so can end the artist's career. "Artistic creativity depends on the acceptance of one's personal mortality," she writes. Fortunately for the artist, these fears can be dealt with through art. Conrad did just that, Segal says, making a "heroic effort to restore his inner world" in his writing. For those who successfully navigate this passage in life, she says, their lives may change, and their work and style as well. They "frequently live to a very ripe old age. Today we could quote as examples Picasso and Henry Moore." Poet James Dickey, who published his first collection of poems at 38, recalls that he realized in mid-life that he would have to leave his successful and enjoyable career in advertising if he were to find enough time for his writing. "I knew I couldn't have it both ways any longer," he told a *Paris Review* interviewer. "I needed a lot more time to do my work and not *their* work. And there is also the feeling of spending your substance, your vital substance, on something that is really not that important"—which, in Dickey's case, was writing ads to sell Coca-Cola. "You just don't want to let yourself go that easily. You can't" (*Writers at Work*, vol. 5, Viking, 1981).

Block Busters

There will be times when the images and ideas just won't come. Or it may be that the gems we do produce can't be translated into a useful form. Many of us are occasionally frustrated by these creative blocks, for reasons that may be hard to get at.

To learn more about blocks, art therapist Carrie W. Crosson, Ph.D., sent a questionnaire to Washington, D.C.-area writers and visual artists, all of them women (*Arts in Psychotherapy*, Winter, 1982). In studying the 271 replies, she found that 78 percent of the respondents had experienced blocks in their work. The most frequently mentioned cause was outside pressures, including work at a job or around the home, childcare, and holidays when the kids are home. Next most often reported was the fear of failure or criticism. Third on the list of blocks was a problem with the creative process itself, such as a need for renewal; not enough time to come up with fresh ideas; working too long and hard at the art; and the cycle of ups and downs that is a part of almost anyone's work. The last two categories of block were lack of self-discipline and physical fatigue (or illness).

Dr. Crosson notes that the nature of blocks seems to change with the artists' ages, as do the artists' ways of approaching a project. Younger people tend to be "spontaneous, intense, and rapid," and might be more susceptible to problems with a lack of self-discipline. Older artists work more slowly, spending time on planning and reworking, and their blocks might respond to allowing more time for the art. At any age, she says, a block can be looked upon as not just a stubborn impediment but a chance to understand the creative process and how to make one's creativity flourish.

At Yale University, researchers Michael V. Barrios and Jerome L. Singer tested the effectiveness of three strategies in overcoming creative blocks. They gathered subjects by running newspaper ads offering help in removing blocks, not just in the arts but in science and in careers. The people who responded were randomly assigned to one of three treatments.

Subjects in the *Waking Imagery* group were led to a quiet room with soft lighting. With eyes closed, they were guided through three sessions of conscious imagery, and encouraged to form mental images in their waking dreams. Once they succeeded in doing this, they were asked to picture their blocks and then to allow themselves to have three conscious dreams of up to two minutes each. Finally, the subjects were told that every night for the next week, they would dream about their blocks, with total recall of these dreams upon awakening.

The *Hypnotic Dream* subjects were also taken to a quiet, dimly lit room, but after they closed their eyes they were led through a relaxation exercise and then listened for 15 minutes to an "environmental tape" of computer-simulated bell tones. The subjects were then asked to form three dream images, and the sessions continued the same as the Waking Imagery sessions, above.

The *Rational Discussion* subjects were shown to a well-lit

room, where they met an experimenter who said that his job would be "to act as a relatively neutral person who will help you focus your thinking in a logical, orderly way." As the two discussed the block, for up to an hour, the experimenter directed the subject's own exploration of possible solutions.

To determine what good each method accomplished, the researchers later interviewed the subjects and asked them to rate how satisfied they were with the resolution of their particular blocks. As the researchers suspected, the most effective method proved to be Waking Imagery, followed by Hypnotic Dream, and then Rational Discussion. They conclude that imagery may resolve blocks in a way that rational approaches cannot.

Not everybody stands to benefit equally, though. Those from the Waking Imagery group who said they were most satisfied with the help they received tended to have scored low levels on a measure of "dysphoric daydreaming" that was taken before the treatment; that is, they were relatively untroubled by guilt or anxiety when daydreaming in focusing and maintaining their attention.

Among those for whom imagery had been helpful was a college professor who was up for tenure but had been unable to write articles in her subject area. Through imagery she was able to adopt a "playful approach" to her writing, and soon thereafter finished an article that was scheduled for publication in a professional journal. A painter overcame a block that had persisted for several years, ever since she had been unable to return to a troublesome painting. She finished the painting, and resumed her work. A writer blocked on producing fiction learned to develop characters through hypnotic dreaming. And an architect daunted at having to propose a design for a center for the handicapped found that guided imagery enabled fresh design ideas to surface.

Booze and the Muse

A popular antidote to creative blocks has been alcohol. By priming his creative pump each dawn with a glass of wine, Belgian novelist Georges Simenon drank and wrote his way through hundreds of novels. But while alcohol is as much a tool for some as pencil and paper, others produce book after book without a drop. Novelist and short-story writer Joyce Carol Oates, who is among the most prolific and imaginative of American authors, does not drink. Nor does she take mind-stimulating drugs, nor even an occasional cup of tea. All are too high-powered for her, she says.

Can alcohol really make a difference? That is the question posed by psychiatrist Donald W. Goodwin, M.D., in his article, "The Muse and the Martini" (*Journal of the American Medical Association*, April 2, 1973). "If it does—a large if—here are two ways it might do so. It may help in starting and help in stopping," he writes. That is, some authors come to rely on alcohol when they are held back by anxiety or simply the lack of something they care very much to express; and others apparently feel they need a drink to calm down *after* a bout of writing.

Starting is the larger problem. "Many rely on ritual," observes Dr. Goodwin. "Hemingway sharpened 20 pencils. Willa Cather read a passage from the Bible. Thomas Wolfe roamed the streets. Another novelist, an agnostic, got down on his knees and started the working day with a prayer.

"Others drink."

Of the six Americans who have received the Nobel Prize for literature, four were alcoholics. The drinking habits of famous hard-drinking authors are well known, even celebrated. In Costello's, a Manhattan tavern, two pieces of a briar cane are mounted above the back bar. There's no label on the wall by way of explanation, but the story is well known. Ernest Hemingway, a heavy-drinking author, boasted to John O'Hara, another, that he could break O'Hara's sturdy cane over his own head, and proceeded to do so.

Dr. Goodwin suggests that alcohol may serve writers as a lens that makes life seem more profound, more significant—and therefore better material for a novel or story. Poet A. E. Housman would drink a pint of beer at lunch and go for a walk, a fortuitous combination that caused to "flow into my mind, with sudden and unaccountable emotion, sometimes a line or two of verse, sometimes a whole stanza. . . ." Essayist E. B. White found that a dry martini was a good solvent for an occasional writer's block. "Alcohol silences the critic" in one's self, observes Dr. Goodwin.

He also acknowledges that alcohol is a powerful, habit-forming drug that can blunt judgment, erase memory, and cause physical illness. Norman Mailer, he relates, once said, "My brain isn't as good as it was years ago. Drinking wrecked half my brain." F. Scott Fitzgerald, when stuck halfway into *Tender Is the Night*, tried treating his block with drink and, by his own admission, spoiled the novel. Edgar Allan Poe drank heavily and experienced delirium tremens, or alcoholic psychosis. Simenon, after writing on beer, wine, cider, whisky, brandy, and grog for decades, switched to Coca-Cola one day in 1949, with only an occasional hard drink thereafter so that abstinence wouldn't seem like "an obsession." After a nervous trial at writing sober, he found he didn't need alcohol after all.

The effect of alcohol on creativity is a popular subject, but little experimental study has been directed at it. Three researchers from Florida State University conducted a test with 40 college students, all of them social drinkers (*Addictive Behaviors*, vol. 9, no. 4, 1984). The subjects were divided into four groups: Of those who were told they were getting vodka and tonic, half did and half got straight tonic; and of those who were told they were getting tonic, half did and half got a mixed drink. Before the test, the subjects were asked whether or not they thought alcohol would enhance their creativity. Then, after taking portions of the Torrance Tests of Creative Thinking, they were asked to rate the creativity of their performances, and also to estimate the quantity of alcohol they had just consumed.

The researchers concluded that alcohol did not have a significant effect on the subjects' creativity. They do note, however, that while their tests involved perception and motor control, an earlier study focusing on *verbal* creativity did associate greater verbal originality with drinking. In this experiment, with 32 college males, Francis J. Hajcak found that originality was counteracted by a reduced ability to apply these responses "to an appropriate solution" (*Dissertation Abstracts International*, vol. 36, 1976).

The Florida study turned up a curious finding: Although all

subjects performed pretty much the same, whether or not they had consumed alcohol, those who were high rated themselves to be more creative than did those who were straight. This was true not only of those who actually received alcohol, but also of those controls who were *told* their tonic water was spiked. There may be a measure of benefit in this side effect, the researchers conclude. When people rate their work more generously, they are less apt to be discouraged by their perfectionism, and more likely to value their instincts.

Thinking Laterally for Better Creativity

Can a person really learn to think more creatively? Yes, and one particular program is now taught in schools and businesses around the world. "Lateral thinking" is part of the curriculum in schools in the United Kingdom, Bulgaria, Venezuela, and Japan. And as proof that you *can* teach old dogs new cognitive tricks, IBM and General Foods are among the companies that have hired consultants to teach lateral thinking to executives.

Lateral thinking is the brainchild of Edward de Bono. His credentials suggest that he must be able to exercise his mind with some facility. A native of the Mediterranean island nation of Malta, he graduated from medical school there at age 21, went on to pick up two doctorates, and has taught at Oxford, Cambridge, and Harvard universities.

Thinking is a difficult skill to teach, finds Dr. de Bono, the man who has probably published more books on the subject than anyone living. As soon as you start to talk about thinking, he says, other people will assume you are suggesting their thinking power isn't up to snuff—"or, worse, that your own thinking is better." (In fact Dr. de Bono has admitted that he doesn't rate himself as a particularly great thinker.)

A problem with the way most of us think, he says, is that we don't tend to the all-important first step in coming up with new information—perception. We're in a rush to reach step number two, the processing of what we perceive.

Lateral thinking emphasizes perception by involving skills for looking at the world in different ways. People resist having to learn these skills, de Bono finds, because they believe that thinking should come naturally, like running or whistling. He points out that resistance is common in learning other skills as well. For example, people can learn to type with two fingers quite quickly. But unless pressed (usually by a class) to use the other eight fingers, they probably will stay at that plateau of ability. Similarly, most of us are two-fingered thinkers, claims Dr. de Bono, in *Teaching Thinking* (Temple Smith, 1976). We rely on prejudice, dogma, and slogans rather than using our brains more fully.

Lateral thinking requires people to direct their attention over a wide field of experience. This flexible point of view may be more valuable to you than a huge bank of knowledge. People put too much stake in assembling all the information they can, Dr. de Bono believes. Psychologist Abraham Maslow agrees, saying that traditional methods of teaching facts don't acknowledge the rate at which the world is now changing. "What's the use of teaching facts?" he asks. "Facts become obsolete so darned fast!" Techniques, too, are old by the time they can be introduced in the classroom. "MIT, for instance, no longer teaches engineering *only* as the acquisition of a series of skills, because practically all the skills that the professors of engineering learned when they were in school have now become obsolete."

Dr. de Bono writes, "The idea that you should read as much as you can in a research field is a great misconception." In fact, he has suggested that researchers work in teams, with one concentrating on the available technical literature and the other taking the time to improvise and invent. (This is much like the strategy of using both halves of the brain on a problem.)

To sketch the program de Bono has developed, here are several of the exercises that he describes in his seminars and books.

Exercises in Lateral Thinking

If you like to read mysteries, you have probably practiced one technique already: challenging assumptions. In order to come up with the guilty person before the author gives it away at the end of the book, you've got to question the apparent evidence and motives. Traditionally, the author will try to place the reader on the wrong trail, while dropping clues that, if heeded, will lead to the actual villain.

Dr. de Bono says that we can learn to adopt this same shrewd, challenging habit in approaching problems. All too often we fall back on stale thinking patterns (or clichéd ideas, as he puts it). In *Lateral Thinking*, he gives the following problem and solution as an example.

A landscaper is told to plant four trees so that each tree is 20 feet from each of the others. If you try to plot this out on a piece of paper, you soon realize that it can't be done—not in two dimensions, anyway. Two trees will always be farther apart than the rest. The solution lies in making use of the third dimension: Place one tree at the top of a steep hill so that it will be brought closer to the one opposite, relative to those on either side.

"That's cheating," someone might say, to which Dr. de Bono would respond that uncreative thinkers have a preconceived notion of bounds which can't be transgressed—whereas to think creatively is to at least test the boundary, if not to step well over it.

How can you encourage yourself to look for slightly off-the-wall alternatives? Dr. de Bono himself allows that this search does not come naturally to most people. We normally grab the first good answer to come along.

The first step is to give up this habit of jumping on the most obvious answer, and take time instead to scout for alternatives. And this, after all, is what creativity is all about: coming up with an idea that other people just didn't see. You know you're doing something right when you find yourself producing solutions that cause people to stop short and exclaim, "Why, of course!"

If you have trouble keeping from running with the first idea that pops into your head, try Dr. de Bono's idea of assigning yourself a quota of possible alternatives, perhaps four or five. He writes in *New Think* (Basic Books, 1968) that, "No matter how absurd the forced interpretations may seem, the quota must be filled." As in a brainstorming session, you have to overcome self-consciousness about generating ideas that in other circumstances might be embarrassingly strange. But with practice, a person becomes more comfortable with the self-imposed quota.

Beware of Mental Habit

Here is a graphic example of how some problems can be solved by going beyond habitual thinking and ordinary assumptions. Below is a grid of nine dots. See if you can connect all of them using just four straight lines and without lifting your pen or pencil from the paper.

The answer lies in considering the space surrounding the square described by the grid. That is, if you restrict yourself to lines that begin and end with a dot, you simply can't do it.

Here's the answer:

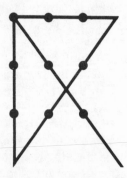

It also takes time to generate four or five possible solutions. We instinctively acknowledge the wisdom of taking time when we say we'll "sleep on" a particularly tough decision.

On those occasions when your brain just isn't up to spinning novel approaches, try interjecting an element of chance by playing with the problem. Dr. de Bono says that playing is in fact "an experiment with chance." And we all know how to play, don't we?

Not really. It is a skill that turns rusty. And it won't do to force yourself to play. "It must be true purposeless play without design and direction," Dr. de Bono says.

You can borrow a little playfulness from the world outside your mind, by picking random words out of the dictionary in hopes that they might spark an idea. Or read a random sentence out of a book—any book—that you pull down from the shelf. Or wander the aisles of a library or hardware store. This allows the world to brainstorm, in effect: to offer words and images that wouldn't otherwise have come to your attention. This course has a relatively low probability of producing a gem of an idea. And it may take some practice before you can overcome the feeling that you're wasting time. You may very well be, of course, but that's all part of the speculative game of lateral thinking.

Brainstorming

There is nothing new in the observation that two heads are better than one: People can spark ideas off each other. But the group-think technique termed brainstorming is relatively recent, having been first described by New York ad executive Alex Osborn in his book, *Your Creative Power* (Scribner's, 1948).

The principle that distinguishes brainstorming from just getting together and talking is that the session begins with a stage in which anything goes. All ideas are allowed a chance, even ones that appear frivolous or outright dumb. This ensures that contributors aren't as apt to feel inhibited about saying something stupid. What's more, the growing list of ideas will help to trigger new and better ones.

Once the ideas have been aired and written down, the

evaluating stage can begin. Only then are the contributions picked apart by the group. As simple as this sounds, it really is radically different from the usual, reflexive style of discussion, in which each idea is either pounced on or praised as it leaves its contributor's mouth. The result can be a creativity block—just as happens to writers when they are so critical of their words that they can't even squeeze out a paragraph before tossing the page in the wastebasket.

You can apply the brainstorming technique to your individual efforts. Allow your ideas to reach a piece of paper, without judging them. Include ridiculous-sounding ideas too, because they may set off a new and better line of thinking. Write rapidly, either in single words or in phrases. Spelling and neatness don't count, because attention to them may gum up your mental gears. When you've exhausted your supply of ideas, it's time to be judgmental. Go over the list, pick the most promising items, and build on them.

Visit Your Unconscious Mind

You can also help yourself to be more creative by giving your imagination occasional workouts. This may mean nothing more than encouraging your mind to produce imaginary movies, and then playing with the images until they become available as sources for your work—whether that be a painting or problems on the job or in daily life.

It is said that Einstein hit upon the theory of relativity while imagining himself flying along at the speed of light. Another often-stated example of the practical power of imagery is that of the German chemist Kekulé, who happened to be dreaming when he discovered that the molecules of benzene are arranged in a circle. And the Italian composer Tartini dreamed that he handed his violin to the devil, who then played a piece that Tartini later turned into his "Devil Sonata."

When you sketch images in your visual imagination, try reinforcing them by bringing in the other senses as well. Rather than simply picturing yourself lying on a beach, listen to the surf; smell the salty air; feel the sand's texture beneath your body and the sun's warmth on your topside.

Roni Beth Tower of Yale University describes imagery as a period of incubation in which thoughts are allowed to come and go, to recombine in novel ways, without editing from you.

An imagery session can begin simply with the memory of a smell, instead of a visual setting. For example, by sensing the tarry odor of creosote, you might be able to summon up the image of walking along an ocean pier, its smell liberated by the heat of the midsummer sun. And then one image can be allowed to lead to another.

Of course, simply letting your imagination take wing won't necessarily lead you to a work of art, Tower points out. Among the problems that may come up are unfocused daydreaming, fantasies that bring on guilt ("I shouldn't be thinking these bizarre thoughts"), and difficulty telling a useful image from a not-so-useful one. Nevertheless, many people have found imaging to be a useful skill, one worth developing.

If you find you have trouble taking walks through the paths of your imagination, you might try listening to a tape of guided imagery. Either buy a prerecorded tape, or make your own. Several suggestions are given in the book *In the Mind's Eye*, by Arnold Lazarus, Ph.D. (Guilford Press, 1977). He offers these specific tips for encouraging a string of vivid images.

First, you've got to relax, by whatever method works best for you: a walk or a run before your imagery session; progressive relaxation, in which you alternately tense and relax muscle groups, starting with your toes; yoga; meditation; and so on.

Second, close your eyes. Most people find that images are clearest if their eyes are closed, says Dr. Lazarus. One reason for this may be that there simply are fewer visual distractions; it can be tough to summon up that tropical beach when you're staring at the wallpaper in your living room. Another reason is that alpha brain waves, which are associated with a relaxed, pleasant state of mind, seem to be produced less generously when the eyes are open, according to George Fritz, Ed.D., a therapist who uses biofeedback-guided imagery in treating a wide range of ailments.

Do what you can to ensure that you won't be interrupted. Put a note on your door that you won't be available until a certain time; take the phone off the hook; do your daily errands beforehand so that guilty, time-urgent thoughts won't intrude.

Some artists and writers have experimented with biofeedback monitors that signal when the brain enters states rich in imagery. Perhaps you've occasionally felt yourself slip into a creative reverie—a semiconscious state in which your mind is dealing with images rather than strings of words. Biofeedback pioneer Elmer Green found that when he entered such states, a brain wave detector reported that he was producing theta waves, the low-frequency waves that tend to occur in the drowsy moments before sleep. At the Menninger Foundation in Topeka, Kansas, he and his wife and co-researcher Alyce Green came up with a regimen that they thought might help a person to slip into such reveries at will. Subjects were trained in yoga, breathing exercises, meditation, and autogenic training (in which the mind, emotions, and body are quieted through imagery). The subjects were then scheduled for regular sessions with a monitor that would feed back an audible signal when brain waves shifted to a theta pattern. A problem that came up was the depth of the theta state: People would drift into semiconsciousness, and weren't able to retrieve the images they experienced. The remedy was to have a subject hold a forearm vertically, with elbow supported, so that a position-sensitive switch on the hand would sound a door chime if the arm was allowed to drop below a certain point.

The feedback sessions in the lab served to teach subjects how to recognize when they were drifting into a theta state of mind. But also important were sessions at home, without the equipment, in which subjects practiced bringing on the state, staying in it, and finally recalling the images which poured forth (for an exercise you can try at home, see chapter 5). One subject found that she was having "vivid, spontaneous" images during relaxed moments of the day.

Most of the subjects were college students, rather than scientists or artists, and it is not surprising that the images that proved helpful to them were associated not with scientific or aesthetic insights, but with everyday personal relationships and emotional issues—the problems apt to be most central for a young man or woman in college. So, it seems that creative imagery can help us in any walk of life.

Other Mind-Expanding Possibilities

Each year, dozens of new books, tape courses, and seminars promise to tell you how to program your brain for super-powered thinking, with the fringe benefit of great success on the job. No attempt to survey them will be made here, but one of the most visible of the lot, "The Neuropsychology of Achievement," will serve as an example. This is a cassette course that can best be described as Dale Carnegie gone holographic. It was based on research from Stanford University which suggests that our memories are stashed not in little cellular pigeonholes, but in holograms formed by intersecting waves of energy. (A hologram is a three-dimensional image that floats in midair.)

The course tells how to tap your memory bank by taking advantage of an instinctive reflex that takes place when you try to remember something—glancing to one side or the other. The "Neuropsychology" program says that we can gain access to a particular kind of memory (visual, tactile, and so on) by directing our eyes in a particular direction.

Try this test. Summon up the memory of your childhood bedroom, its lighting in particular. Note the direction in which your eyes seem to gaze as you search for this visual image.

Now recall as best you can the physical sensation of bodysurfing, or schussing down a ski slope, or swimming underwater, whichever comes to mind more clearly. Again, note the direction of your gaze.

If you are right-handed, this theory has it, your eyes look to the upper left when the memory is summoning visual material. And memories of bodily sensation are said to involve a glance to the lower right. (For lefties, the eyes look to the opposite side.)

This program attempts to put these findings to a practical end. Its developer, Steven DeVore, says he discovered that we can consciously search our mental files by steering our eyes this way and that. The "success" angle comes in here: You can make

Southpaw Pluses and Minuses

Left-handed people seem to have earned a measure of prejudice in many societies. In fact, the word "sinister" has as its root the Latin *sinistra*, meaning "left"; and our word "dexterity" evolved from the Latin *dexter*, or "right," because the right hand has long been considered the more dexterous of the two. This could be passed off as so much superstition if handedness were simply a matter of chance. But take a look at this chart of characteristics that have been identified as occurring more often among the left-handed. Clearly, being left-handed goes beyond an occasional difficulty in using right-handed can openers and the like.

These lists don't mean that lefties are any worse off than the right-handed majority—merely that they tend to have their own particular mix of talents and problems.

Pluses

Superior spatial intelligence
Higher maths aptitude
Higher incidence of athletes, artists, architects,
    engineers, mathematicians, and musicians
Less prone to senile dementia
Stroke victims regain speech faster because language
    facility is located on both sides of brain

Minuses

Autism, dyslexia, stuttering
Immune diseases
Allergies (asthma, eczema, hay fever)
Infections
Hypertension
Migraine
Early grey hair

Creative Lefties

Lefties seem to flock to fields that rely on spatial intelligence.

In a study published in *Perceptual and Motor Skills* (vol. 48, 1979), John Peterson, of the University of Cincinnati, looked at the percentage of left-handers among 1,045 undergraduate students in a number of majors. (Handedness was defined by which hand the subject used to draw.) While the overall percentage of lefties was 9.38, a high of 14.89 percent were music majors; 12.24 percent were in design, architecture, and art; and 10.67 percent were in engineering. Fewest lefties were found in nursing and the sciences (just above 4 percent each). Another study found that not only are lefties well represented among architecture students, but they also tend to have a better chance of making it to graduation.

visualizations of success more powerful by using eye movement to bring the senses to bear on whatever you're trying to "program" into your brain. As DeVore applies the method to public speaking, for example, "You should create an extremely vivid image of what you'll look like as a successful speaker. You should also design an image of the sounds that are associated with reaching that goal, and the bodily feelings, the smells, and the emotions accompanying it." And as for bad habits that you want to shake, the program would have you associate them with the image of a demon, which is then done in by a visualization.

"The Neuropsychology of Achievement" and other programs on audio and video cassettes may be more accessible to some people than how-to books. In this particular program, the narrator's voice is almost irresistibly mellifluous, and the handsome packaging can't help but inspire confidence in the technique.

Creativity Tips

Ultimately, each of us is left to find the routines and thoughts that allow our creativity to flourish. What works wonders for another person may leave you totally uninspired. For example, poet Elizabeth Bishop once tried to bring on inspirational dreams by eating lots of Roquefort cheese each night before going to bed. For German poet Johann Schiller, nothing worked so well as a desk drawer filled with rotten apples. And French author Marcel Proust retreated to a cork-lined workroom.

If cheese, apples, and cork don't do it for you, experiment with the suggestions that follow. Don't assume that creativity comes naturally. It may take a conscious effort to switch from your standard mode of thought to a speculative mode. The mind, like any other part of the body, likes to be comfortable, and it finds familiar, well-worn ideas as comfortable as a favorite old pair of slippers. Thinking expert Edward de Bono warns this means we may have to purposefully be "deliberate and artificial" in order to try different approaches. The result can be a lot of inappropriate, even foolish-sounding ideas. But that's okay. Says Dr. de Bono, "The need to be right all the time is the biggest bar there is to new ideas." He tells a story as an example of how mind habits interfere with thinking in new situations. A man is tired of constantly letting his pregnant cat in and out, and he hits upon the solution of cutting a hole in the door. He is so pleased with his idea that, as soon as the cat bears kittens, he cuts a second, kitten-size hole in the door.

We've all cut our kitten-size trapdoors, as a result of applying once-sound ideas to a problem that since has changed. The next few pages suggest how to avoid these ruts.

Don't let logic bog you down. Logic has its value—as a means of checking the validity of your new ideas. But logic sits on creative thoughts because it demands them to be orderly and to make good sense.

That's why a logical problem solver makes a beeline in the most obvious direction. He or she makes no allowance for farfetched, chancy alternatives—odd ideas that may lead to great discoveries. Rocket propulsion might never have been developed if Robert Goddard had accepted the logical conviction of fellow scientists that a rocket could not work in outer space because the escaping gases would have nothing to push against. That was sound thinking, based as it was on current scientific theory; but it happened to be wrong. The rocket came to be only because Goddard allowed himself to skip a logical step in developing it. Einstein emphasized the role played by intuition in science. "There is no logical way to the discovery of [complex scientific] laws," he said. "There is only the way of intuition, which is helped by a feeling for the order lying behind appearance."

If you have trouble letting your intuition play, Dr. de Bono suggests trying to deliberately pick a wrong assumption and then proceeding from there.

When a problem refuses to budge, flip it upside down. For example, the engineers who designed the Citroen automobile took advantage of the car's adjustable hydraulic suspension in this ingenious way. Rather than jack up the 3,000-pound car to change a flat, the Citroen owner merely places a stand under the car and then retracts the wheels. The car doesn't move—the wounded wheel does.

Think of the problem visually. When you use certain words and phrases to the point that they suddenly stop making sense, shift to visual thinking. This calls on spatial intelligence, believed to be centered in the right brain hemisphere, while verbal skills are centered in the left. If possible, go to the site of the problem and just have a look around.

Think of the problem abstractly. Yes, this is the opposite of the preceding suggestion. But it works in the same way, through a shift to another style of looking at things. A common example is to make lists of positive and negative factors when faced with a tough decision. Plans and outlines also serve to pare a complex situation down to its skeleton. Mathematics is one such tool, but it is so abstract that it may be too specialized for the grey areas of day-to-day problems.

SPEAK TO A FRIEND

Speak your mind. Another way to put life back into terms that have become meaningless is to vocalize them—to yourself, to a tape recorder, or to a receptive listener. Just as some novelists read their work aloud to test its quality, so you can judge your ideas by speaking them.

Decide you're going to come up with a certain number of solutions. That is, force yourself to invent four or five new ideas, even if some sound preposterous to you. Suspend judgment and allow yourself to play with the possibilities.

Don't fret if you don't have all the facts. Dr. de Bono says that people tend to incorrectly assume that the more data they can pile up, the better the chance they'll come up with a sound idea. We are taught this bias in school: to value knowledge over thinking. But too much knowledge can be crippling, finds Dr. de Bono. "The brain is a good computer simply because it has a bad memory." And knowledge tends to become stale quickly, especially in technological areas. "The engineering schools are torn by this realization," writes psychologist Abraham Maslow. Schools must help a student to become "a new kind of human being who is comfortable with change ... who is able to improvise. . . ."

Stop worrying about the past and future. That's a tall order, especially for the habitual worrywarts among us. See the previous chapter for a number of ways to reduce anxiety. And for now, consider the words of Eric M. Bienstock, Ph.D., a New York thinking consultant who has given many corporate seminars. He points out that worry about the past is *guilt*, straight and simple, and that worry about the future is *anxiety*; either emotion can gum up the creative machinery. While a moderate level of arousal may enhance memory and alertness, a big dose of adrenaline can interfere with memory, cause unpleasant and distracting physical symptoms (loss of breath, queasiness in the stomach, hands that sweat and tremble), and even dilate the pupils of the eyes enough to interfere with reading. Understandably, a person in such a fix finds it difficult to concentrate. Abraham Maslow points out that when the work is going well, our thoughts of the past and future tend to drop away. We put on hold any nervous plans and worries. In contrast, by trying too hard, you can scare elusive ideas back down into the unconscious mind. Remember that brainstorms often happen when least expected, not when planned for. Physicist Albert Einstein said that his best ideas popped into his head while shaving in the morning.

Try not to edit ideas as they are born. An often repeated tenet of creative writing is to put off editing (or judging) your material until it has at least enough time to reach paper or VDU screen. Give yourself a chance. If you're too quick to pounce on your mistakes, your silliness, your fond dreams, then the consequence can be an extremely frustrating creative block. Instead, you have to let the work "have its way," says Maslow, like athletes who find they play best when they just "let it happen."

Be receptive to the creative springs within you. They bubble in our dreams, and with practice you may be able to recall pieces of these fantastic stories upon awakening (a bedside notebook helps here). The peace of a long-distance drive or the solitude of a leisurely walk may allow ideas to surface. Writers and artists have a special interest in making the most of such moments, of course. They may keep journals to save scraps of fantasy and imagery. They often jealously guard private times of the day so that the mind is kept clear for whatever may come to it. For some, it helps to prime the creative flow by being with other creative people, to visit galleries and museums.

A little tension may be all to the good. It's unsettling to try out new ideas. If you are producing something genuinely new, then obviously you can't be sure of the outcome. Among those artists who have been named as particularly plagued by uncertainty are Alberto Giacometti, Paul Cézanne, Vincent Van Gogh, and Henri Matisse. Poet Stephen Spender says that a writer's struggles may lend the work a dynamic quality that is lacking in the more polished work of an artist who has already mastered the skills of the trade and is no longer taking great risks.

Too Calm to Create?

Does meditation nurture creativity? One meditator says not. Rollo May found that his customary 20-minute sessions were a good way to wind down after a bout of writing, but that the words just wouldn't come if he meditated *before* sitting down to write. That's because the mental calm, as good as it felt, removed the inner stresses that drove him to write in the first place. There seems to be an optimal level of arousal for creativity: Too little, and you sit there with a pleasant smile; too much, and you pace about in a state of mental disorganization.

Be childlike. As children, most of us had a good measure of creativity. And because kids tend to be open, trusting, and unselfconscious, the products of this creativity flow out freely, in a way that's beautiful to watch.

In fact, creativity has been called an act of "voluntary regression"—a journey to an earlier psychological terrain. Picasso said that, after learning to draw on a level with Raphael, he had to discover how to draw like a child. Voluntary regression is a sign of a psychologically healthy person. But slipping back into an uninhibited, innocent state can be frightening to some people, says Maslow. If they can't let themselves go and insist on remaining in control, they may remain influenced by what the work *should* look like.

You can learn to will yourself into a creative mood. Be silly, advises Dr. Bienstock. Be innocent, childlike, says Maslow. He points out that creative people tend to keep alive a childlike side, a playful part of the personality that is allowed to survive into adulthood. Older people may find that one of the benefits of aging is a measure of independence from the opinions of others.

Take the chance that you'll stumble occasionally. It can take courage to risk looking silly. You have to accept the possibility that your poems, paintings, or ideas may strike others as naive, stupid-sounding, or just plain bad. Maslow says that "most studies of creative people have reported one or another version of courage: stubbornness, independence, self-sufficiency, a kind of arrogance, strength of character."

Allow your sense of humor to play, too. Finding humor in daily life can help keep your mind flexible, and a brain has to be limber if it's to stay creative. We are made to laugh when we are tickled by a sudden shift from our usual, everyday perspective to a new way of looking at things.

Realize that creating can be hard work. An inspiration may just float down out of the blue. But great ideas tend to visit those who have already invested plenty of interest and time in that particular field. For example, a brilliant idea for improving the efficiency of a carburetor isn't apt to pop into the head of someone who couldn't care less about the mechanics of the internal combustion engine.

Give your muse some peace and quiet. These are precious commodities to most of us, and may be hard to find. Rollo May suspects that a life which is full of television, radio, and hustle and bustle will probably lack opportunities for insights to present themselves to the conscious mind. (In fact, some people use constant noise and activity to keep uncomfortable thoughts bottled up.)

Do you have a private retreat to which you can go when you want to spin thoughts? Artists and writers tend to put a lot of importance on preparing their special places for creating.

Allow yourself plenty of time. Another important ingredient of creative works is time, and many careers in the arts bog down for lack of it. William Schuman, director of the MacDowell Colony for artists in New Hampshire, said that he jealously guards the time he devotes to composing music. "I realized that if I wanted to be a composer, I'd have to protect that time." He has allocated 600 to 1,000 hours per year to writing music, and keeps track of this precious resource to the minute. If Schuman has to leave his studio for a two-minute phone call in the house, he makes note of the time lost and makes it up later.

Take advantage of chance. When your mind runs out of new approaches to a problem, allow chance to have a hand in directing your thoughts. Make your mind receptive to accidental discoveries, to suggestions provided by sights, smells, and sounds around you.

When coming up with a design for a machine to test lung function, Dr. de Bono wandered the aisles of a Woolworth's department store, hoping that an object would spark a new approach. The eventual solution was stimulated by a plastic flute—a simple enough object, but one that set off a chain of creative thoughts. The same purpose is served by wandering through the stacks of a library—not with Dewey decimals written on a little slip of paper to guide you, but with an open mind. Singer and songwriter Joni Mitchell says she has generated new ideas by opening a book at random and reading a passage. Similarly, Dr. de Bono suggests picking random words from a dictionary as a means of encouraging new thoughts to surface. Perhaps you've had the experience of pausing when writing, and then finding that an overheard scrap of conversation provides just the phrase or inspiration you need to continue. Novelist William Burroughs introduced chance into his manuscripts by cutting them up and recombining the pieces.

Brainstorming is a system for taking advantage of stray, uncensored thoughts as they bounce off a group of people. The key is to avoid the reflex of ruling out thoughts that don't immediately seem pertinent, and to grant these thoughts a place on a blackboard so that they have a chance to stimulate new thoughts.

D. N. Perkins, in his book *The Mind's Best Work* (Harvard University Press, 1981), stresses that taking advantage of chance is not a passive activity. Accidents are most apt to benefit the mind that is already preoccupied by a goal. "The use of chance is passive but watchful," says Dr. de Bono. "As our confidence grows, thinking without consciously directing thought becomes easier; as it becomes easier it becomes more effective."

Run or walk your way to greater creativity. There's no guarantee of success here, but it wouldn't hurt to try, according to a study published in *Perceptual and Motor Skills* (February, 1985). Working with college students who had not been runners, the researchers found that twice-weekly running sessions of 20 minutes, kept up for eight weeks, seemed to bring about significant changes in some tests of creativity. The researchers suggest that exercise can improve right-brain performance—an especially important benefit for students, says this study, because schools tend to emphasize academic, left-brain subjects over the arts and physical education.

John Jerome works as a freelance writer, a job that succeeds or founders on the ability to come up with new, workable ideas. "My problem is always concentration," says Jerome. "I don't block, but I do fuzz out, sometimes as soon as 45 minutes, sometimes after three or four hours. As soon as I realize I've gone 10 minutes without working, one of the best things I can do is get some exercise"—not sweat-producing exercise, but 10 or 15 minutes of walking or housecleaning.

Create, or else. Creativity may be a survival trait. In *The Courage to Create*, Rollo May says that we must imagine a better world and then set about to achieve it. Without a creative leap into a heretofore unknown world of peace, this earth may not survive.

Index